OPERA

Johannes Jansen

BARRON'S

Cover photos from top to bottom and left to right:
Theater an der Wien, Theater collection of the University of Köln, Schloss Wahn / Bass Tito
Gobbi asprotagonist in Verdi's *Simone Boccanegra*, Schloss Wahn / Maria Callas, photo,
EMI Classics / The soprano Anna Pauline Milder in Christoph Willibald Gluck's *Orpheus*,
19th century, Schloss Wahn / Program of the Milan Scala staging of *Armide* by Christoph
Willibald Gluck, CONCERTO, Köln / The conductor Ferenc Fricsay in the 1950s in West Berlin,
Schloss Wahn / Carmen-Figurine by Josef Fenneker, Berlin 1949, Schloss Wahn / *L'incorona-
zione di Poppea* in a staging by Jürgen Flimm, Salzburg Festival 1993, photo by Photowerk-
statt Esser/Baus / Scene from Caldara's opera *I Disingannati*, Innsbruck Festival 1993,
photo by Rupert Larl / *Jonny Strikes up* by Ernst Křenek, staging sketch by Johannes Schröder,
Duisburg 1928, Schloss Wahn / Claudio Monteverdi, AKG Berlin / Frieda Hempel and Enrico
Caruso (right) in Gaetano Donizetti's *Love Potion*, Berlin 1910, Schloss Wahn

Back cover photos from top to bottom:
Figurine of Basilio by Hans Strohbach for a Mozart project (*Marriage of Figaro*, 1932),
Schloss Wahn / Stage illustration by Simon Quaglio for Mozart's *Magic Flute*, Munich 1818,
Schloss Wahn / Characters of the Commedia dell'arte as Meissen porcellain figures,
Schloss Wahn

Frontispiece:
Baritone Francisco d'Andrade as Don Giovanni with his servant Leporello (so-called graveyard scene), engraving by Max Slevogt, 1920, Schloss Wahn, © VG Bild-Kunst, Bonn 1998

American text version by: Agents–Producers–Editors, Overath, Germany
Translated by: Marion Kleinschmidt, Bludenz, Austria
Edited by: Bessie Blum, Cambridge, Ma.

First edition for the United States and Canada
published by Barron's Educational Series, Inc., 1998.

First published in Germany in 1998 by
DuMont Buchverlag GmbH und Co. Kommanditgesellschaft, Köln, Federal Republic of Germany

Text copyright © 1998 DuMont Buchverlag GmbH und Co. Kommanditgesellschaft,
Köln, Federal Republic of Germany.

Copyright © 1998 U.S. language translation, Barron's Educational Series, Inc.

All inquiries should be addressed to:
Barron's Educational Series, Inc.
250 Wireless Boulevard
Hauppauge, New York 11788
http://www.barronseduc.com

International Standard Book No.   0–7641–0438–1

Library of Congress Catalog Card No. 98–70746

Printed in Italy by Editoriale Libraria

Content

Preface

A crash course in opera is not an opera guide, much less a substitute for the immediate experience of opera on stage. But it can supplement and deepen one's understanding of both of these. In its cursory tour through history, this book examines not only the essential aspects of the genre and the most important repertoire works, but also deals with striking individual phenomena and aspects such as decoration, costume and stagecraft. In addition to extra pages dedicated to composers like Monteverdi and Wagner, there are also examinations of the recording era and the great opera houses of our time, timetables that make it easier to place works in their historical context, and an index and glossary to help one quickly find names and facts.

The brief, generally understandable presentation which is the goal of this work could not succeed without the integration of myriad illustrations which help bring the themes, figures and venues of four centuries of opera to life. The majority, including previously unpublished sketches of sets, characters, and costumes, are taken from the dramaturgical collection of the University of Cologne, Germany. I would like to express my gratitude to the people in charge of that collection, as well as other sources of pictures and illustrations, who were of help during the research for this book.

Clearly, a single evening at the opera brings us closer to its secrets than any written description, be it ever so animated. Even the fascination of recordings, especially the older sound documents, can only offer a weak approximation of the experience of live voices in a vivid theater atmosphere. This crash course aims to be one thing above all: an invitation to the endless pleasure to be derived from an art form which, more than most others, challenges and delights our senses; provided opera finds its appropriate niche in a cultural landscape increasingly dominated by short-sighted, tight-fisted politics.

Johannes Jansen

The hallmarks of musical history up to 1600

2nd century AD
Hymns of Mesomedes.

350–400
Hymns of St. Ambrosius.

after 600
Gregorian Chant (named after Pope Gregory I).

after 900
Early polyphony.

around 1180
Chants by Hildegard of Bingen.

around 1200
The Maastricht *Easter Play.*

around 1250
Ludus Danielis (religious play based on the Book of Daniel).

around 1280
Le Jeu de Robin et de Marion by Adam de la Halle (secular *singspiel*).

1316
Roman de Fauvel by Gervais du Bus with numerous musical parts.

1475
Bordesholmer Marienklage (religious play for Good Friday).

1501
Ottaviano Petrucci introduces the printing of musical notes by means of separate letters.

1581
Balet comique de la Royne by Baltasar de Beaujoyeulx.

Man and Measure, an anatomical study by Leonardo da Vinci.

A momentous misunderstanding: The spirit of the Renaissance gives rise to opera

The city-states of northern Italy were the main theater for what we call the Renaissance. In rejecting traditional medieval ways of thinking and forms of art, Florence—which together with Venice was the most important commercial center of the region at the end of the 15th century— experienced a cultural highpoint of hitherto unknown dimensions. Based on a pervasive new spirit of optimism arising from an intellectual confrontation with the classical world, a new view of the world emerged for scholars and artists: Man was the measure of all things. One of the most important works of the Florentine philosopher Giovanni Pico della Mirandola, *De hominis dignitate*, dealt with this new concept of human dignity. Even so, in Renaissance Florence, witches were still being persecuted.

This was the time of the great explorations: In 1498 Vasco da Gama found a sea route to India, Christopher Columbus and Amerigo Vespucci discovered the New World of America, and in 1520 through his voyage around the world, Ferdinand Magellan incontrovertibly proved that the earth was round.

The old world order upheld by the Church began to topple, while in the heart of Europe the Reformation dawned and changes in the political situation stepped up their pace and intensity. One of the greatest armed conflicts in Europe, shaking

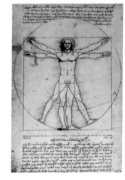

not only the foundations of Italy, was the sacking of Rome by imperial mercenary troops in the year 1527, but both the Peasants' Revolt in Germany and the Turkish conquest of Belgrade were instrumental in destabilizing Europe. In fact, many date the end of the Renaissance to the sacking of Rome, which established the dominance of the House of Habsburg in Italy. Nevertheless, as an intellectual movement, emerging from Italian humanism, the Renaissance continued to influence all areas of art and literature. As late as the end of the 16th century, Renaissance thought made its presence felt in a new musical genre: opera.

Many Florentine scholars and artists, following upon Leonardo da Vinci or Giorgio Vasari, played a part in spurring this new development, among them most notably musicians such as Jacopo Peri, Giulio Caccini, Emilio de' Cavalieri, and Vincenzo Galilei, the renowned musical theorist and father of the famous mathematician and astronomer. But the decisive impetus for opera came from the philologist Girolamo Mei whose rediscovery of three late classical hymns and study of ancient Greek music, *Discorso sopra la musica antica e moderna*, renewed interest in and study of the musical and declamatory art of the classical world.

Mei, Giovanni Bardi, and Galilei were members of the *Camerata*, a society of Florentine poets and musicians who were united in their belief that only monody, that is, solo song with instrumental accompaniment, and not polyphony, was true to the classical Greek ideal of performance. This ideal was derived from the sources available to the Renaissance: the classical Greek tragedies, primarily those by Euripides

The Manifesto of Monody, Vincenzo Galilei's treatise, written in the form of a dialogue, on the advantages of modern music, published in 1581. In polyphony, which was considered outdated, the text was set to music according to the rules of counterpoint alone (*punctus contra punctum*—note against note), and not according to the natural rhythm of speech. The independent vocal melodies, superimposed and intertwined, in effect obscured the text and rendered it meaningless. In monody, as in the choruses of the new style (*stile nuovo*), on the other hand, the comprehensibility of the text was the most important rule of musical composition.

An early Baroque ensemble, consisting of a harpsichord, cornet, harp, lute, and bass viol. (Detail of an engraving by Antonio Tempesta, 1622.)

and Sophocles, and the *Poetics* of Aristotle. The theory of the *Camerata*, however, stood on precarious ground, since the highly complex ancient Greek theories on metrically determined declamation of music and text as an organic unity were not easily or clearly translatable into the modern categories of melody and rhythm; in fact, those few surviving fragments of Greek notation did not allow for exact conclusions. The late Florentine attempt to reconstruct the classical ideal thus remained a highly speculative undertaking. Nonetheless, the attempt itself had far-reaching consequences.

The Florentine *Camerata*

In addition to the composers already named above, poets such as Ottavio Rinuccini and Count Giovanni Bardi also belonged to the *Camerata*. Bardi was a patron of the arts, an author, and a composer, as well as one of the intellectual leaders of this learned circle, which met on a regular basis at his house. Assiduously distancing themselves from the past masters of vocal polyphony who had attained such a high degree of compositional ingenuity and complexity by the mid-16th century, the *Camerata* favored a comparatively simple model of composition: the *monody*. Derived from the Greek word for solo song, the monody was typically performed as *recitar cantando*, patterned after the natural rhythms of speech and emphasizing the emotional quality of the text in its melodic line. The air was accompanied simply by *basso continuo* instruments such as the harpsichord, organ, lute, or chitarrone.

The musical life of wealthy cities like Florence was characterized by the penchant of the noble and patrician families for ostentation; many wished to show off their positions and importance to greatest advantage. Prominent families were continually vying with one another in the sumptuousness of their feasts and celebrations. But ostentation was not confined to the egoism of the nobility, the braggadocio of triumphal processions, the pomp of court masquerades, and the luxury of theatrics; it was equally important to the Church and manifested in elaborate *rappresentazioni sacre* and Latin school dramas which had been performed in monastic schools since the Middle Ages.

The Church of Santa Maria in Vallicella (with the oratory, newly built in 1637). Here, in 1600, *Rappresentazione di anima e di corpo* by Ottavio Rinuccini (text) and Emilio de' Cavalieri (music) was performed for the first time. Although it was a part of the tradition of religious entertainment, suggestive somewhat of the later oratorio, its arias in the *stile recitativo*, its choruses and dance scenes place it intrinsically in the ranks of the early opera.

A Momentous Misunderstanding

The Florentine Camerata

In Vicenza, the Teatro Olimpico, newly built by Andrea Palladio, was ceremoniously opened in 1584. It was the first enclosed theater building to be constructed according to the classical concept of the theater. For the inauguration, an Italian translation of Sophocles' *Edipo Tiranno* (*Oedipus Rex*) was performed. Andrea Gabrieli, the organist of St. Mark's Cathedral in Venice, contributed four large choruses for the gala event. The choral works were written in counterpoint; however, the expressive treatment of the text anticipated the modern style.

In fact, a number of musical-dramatic traditions contributed to the development of the early opera, though clearly the strongest impetus came from court festivities. Opera would remain exclusively a courtly event well into the middle of the 17th century, when the first public opera houses were built in Venice. One particularly splendid event in the pomp-loving Florence of the later 16th century was the marriage of Ferdinand de' Medici to Christine of Lothringen. Among the festivities, which overall lasted many days, was *La Pellegrina*, a comedy by Girolamo Bargagli. Between the different acts, an *intermedio* provided entertainment during scene changes.

In time the amusing *intermedii* grew more popular with the public than the play itself. The

Costume designs by Buontalenti for the Florentine *interludes*, intended for the royal wedding of 1589.

As an intrinsic part of the cultural life of the court, dances were an element of the opera from its very beginnings. This illustration shows the premiere of the *Balet comique de la Royne*, performed in the presence of King Henry III in the Louvre for a wedding in 1581. It is the work of the Italian choreographer and violinist Baltasar de Beaujoyeulx, and is the prototype for the court ballet (*ballet de cour*), combining poetry, music, dance, and scenery, all elements of the later opera. This ballet has survived in print and was revived in 1997 (illustration from the Festival d'Ambronay).

six *intermedii* written for the royal wedding of 1589 were in keeping with the special Florentine tradition: They were elaborately conceived and performed. The architect Bernardo Buontalenti designed the stage scenery, the costumes, and decorations. The plots and characters were drawn from the classical mythology, and these continued to dominate court theatrical performances into the late Baroque period. The tribute to the prince at the beginning of the performance was obligatory. In this particular instance, the allegorical figure of Harmony, with an entourage consisting of Parcae (the Fates), Heroes, and Planets, sang the praises of the wedded couple.

The painstaking efforts and excessive expenditures involved in creating the stage sets were extreme: Cities, celestial worlds, and landscapes appeared and disappeared, luminous flying devices floated through the hall, and, for the fifth interlude, which portrayed the sea goddess Amphitrite riding in a dolphin-drawn carriage made of shells, water pools and fountains were created. Even exotic fragrances permeated the air to round out the sensuous fantasy.

Mirtillo (second from left), the faithful shepherd ("Il pastor fido"; illustration from Venice, 1602). The ten *Bucolica* by the classical Roman poet Vergil, based on the pastoral poetry of the Greek Theocritus, were repeatedly imitated in the 15th and 16th centuries and inspired such dramatic forms as the tragicomedy and the shepherds' plays (*favola pastorale*), which often had musical accompaniment. Verses from Guarini's *Il pastor fido*, which after Tasso's *Aminta* was the most famous pastoral drama of its time, were set to music hundreds of times.

Seven composers worked on the music for the *intermedii,* and dozens of singers and instrumentalists were employed. Among these were Giulio Caccini and Emilio de' Cavalieri, who composed the music to the elaborate final ballet.

Shepherds' plays, ballets, and masques

Arcadia, a mountainous area of the Peloponnesian peninsula, became in Vergil a "locus amoenus," an idyllic place celebrated by generations of poets as the garden of love, friendship, and peace, as well as the home of Pan, the pastoral god of fertility. Arcadia was omnipresent in the courts of the 16th and 17th centuries: Shepherds, lovers, nymphs and satyrs peopled countless shepherds' plays and ballets. In addition, the nobility delighted in convening at rustic feasts, attired in shepherds' costumes. Torquato Tasso in *Aminta* (1573) and Giovanni Batista Guarini in *Il pastor fido* (1590) initiated a new genre with these pastoral plays—the tragicomedy. Similarly, shepherds stories and romances cropped up throughout Europe. The most famous of these was *L'Astrée* (1607–1627), a comprehensive work of about 5,000 pages by Honoré d'Urfé, which the nobility adopted as a guide or manual to true aristocratic behavior.

Influenced by the Pléiade poets (a group of seven 16th century poets who took their name from a similar group in Alexandria, circa 280 BC), French artists, like their counterparts in the Florentine *Camerata*, worked to develop a "musique mesurée à l'antique," in which the precise metrics also determined the ballet choreography. These so-called "ballets de cour" in fact became the main vessels for conveying classical concerns on the stage. Characters were taken from classical mythology and allegorical figures played the leading roles in court ballets, most of which lacked a unifying plot. They were, in effect, opulently staged pageants with elaborate dances in which the nobility and even the king himself participated.

In England such operatic, or pre-operatic, conventions merged with the popular masquerades to form a new genre, the *masque*, again an elaborate, pompous mixture of dance, pantomime, and song in which the court took an active part. The "*antimasque*," a historically somewhat newer offshoot of this genre that soon became a permanent part of all performances, was somewhat more

Orfeo am I, who pursues the steps of Eurydice through this dark plain, which has never yet been entered by mortal man.

Oh, the cheering lights of my eyes, one glance of yours can restore life to me, ah, who refuses to comfort me in my suffering?

You alone, noble God, can grant me aid.

You need not fear me, for I have only the sweet strings of my golden lyre as weapon, which can soften the hardest souls.

Claudio Monteverdi, L'Orfeo, Act III. 1607 ("Orfeo son io …")

Apollo and Daphne, sculpture by Gian Lorenzo Bernini. Next to the Orpheus myth, the story of Daphne, who must protect herself from Apollo's advances, was the most popular subject of early opera. Daphne is the focus of the very first opera, although, unfortunately, the music has been lost. Marco da Gagliano again set this story to music (Mantua, 1608), as did Francesco Cavalli (Venice, 1640). The history of opera in Germany also began with Daphne, although the opera *Daphne* by Heinrich Schütz (Torgau, 1627; text by Martin Opitz) was also lost.

grotesque in character and was left to professional comedians and Moresca dancers.

Orpheus, the prototype of the opera

Tasso and Guarini had modeled their tragi-comedies on Angelo Poliziano's *Favola d'Orfeo*, written in 1480. The Orpheus material that inspired modern pastoral poetry also formed the cornerstone of all operas. With the exception of Jacopo Peri's *Dafne* (1598), from which the libretto and only a few fragments of musical notation survive, all of the earliest operas are based on

Orpheus, the Thracian singer who was able to enchant man and beast, to soften even rocks, and to mollify the powers of the underworld. A tragic version of the myth of Orpheus leading his beloved Eurydice out of the realm of the dead is related in Vergil's *Georgics* and Ovid's *Metamorphoses,* and both Dante and Petrarch conveyed it into modern times. On the threshold of the 17th century, Florentine composers adapted the myth to opera, as so many later composers continued to do, thereby returning Orpheus to his own special medium. From Claudio Monteverdi to Johann Joseph Fux, Christoph Willibald Gluck and Joseph Haydn to Jacques Offenbach and Hans-Werner Henze, composers have continued to be fascinated by the Orpheus myth.

The first attempt to portray this dramatic subject matter, fittingly in the form of *recitar cantando,* or vocal recitation, was undertaken by Jacopo Peri. His production of *Euridice* included a number of compositions by Giulio Caccini, who later composed a completely new version of the text by Rinuccini (who had already written the libretto to *Dafne*). As a result, Caccini declared himself the first to bring a work out in print in the new *stile rappresentativo.*

In the year 1597, Orazio Vecchi's *L'Amfiparnaso* appeared. Vecchi and his librettist Giulio Cesare Croce used themes from pastoral poetry and from the *commedia dell'arte*, weaving them with great virtuosity into a dramatically loose musical comedy. It was not staged, but performed as a sequence of five-part madrigals. Although Adriano Banchieri was a follower of Vecchi, the madrigal comedy did not survive as a genre.

Euridice, by Jacopo Peri and Giulio Caccini. The edition of the oldest preserved opera contains only the vocal parts and the bass notes of the accompaniment (*basso continuo*); details about instrumentation are missing.

Claudio Monteverdi (1567–1643).

As one of many events celebrating the marriage of Maria de' Medici to Henry IV of France, Peri's *Euridice* was performed for the first time on October 6, 1600. Because of its spectacular success, this premiere marked the beginning of a new chapter in music history. However great the fame at that time of Peri and Caccini, who were both also excellent singers, both have been eclipsed by Monteverdi and his *L'Orfeo*, from the year 1607.

The most influential family in Mantua, the home of Vergil, was the royal house of the Gonzagas, whose power and importance were comparable to the Medicis in Florence and the Estes in Ferrara. The Gonzagas rose to power through the military and prided themselves not only on the many generals in their family but also on the great patrons of the arts, who even persuaded Angelo Poliziano to reside at the court of Mantua for some time. In 1590, at the age of 23, Claudio Monteverdi was employed by the Gonzagas as a violinist; twelve years later he was appointed court conductor.

Monteverdi came from Cremona, where he was a pupil of Marc' Antonio Ingegneri, the cathedral choirmaster. By the time he was 15, he had already published a collection of motets, which were soon followed by his first two collections of madrigals (he produced nine in all). During his ten years as composer and conductor at the court of Mantua (his tenure came to an abrupt end in 1612 with the change of sovereign), Monteverdi composed, among many other works, the opera *Arianna*, from which only the famous lamento survives, and the *Ballo delle ingrate*. The occasion for their composition was the marriage of Francesco Gonzaga to Margherita of Savoy in 1608. Ottavio Rinuccini, who wrote the dramas on which these operas were based, was in charge of the festival productions. Monteverdi's first opera, *L'Orfeo*, on the other hand, based on a text of his friend and fellow court official Alessandro Striggio, was not primarily intended for a specific court festivity. It was first to be performed for a group of so-called insiders, members of the *Accademia degli invaghiti*, an institution somewhat like the *Camerata* in Florence. It was only because of *L'Orfeo's* great initial success that it was performed shortly thereafter at the court and for the public again in Mantua.

In contrast to Rinuccini's *Euridice*, Monteverdi and Striggio adhered closely to Poliziano's five-act, classically structured drama and kept the tragic conclusion of the *Favola d'Orfeo*: When Orpheus journeyed to the underworld to retrieve his dead wife Eurydice, the gods forbade him to look around at her until they had left Hades, but in the tragic tradition of Vergil and Ovid, Orpheus turned around to look back at Eurydice, thus losing her again, this time forever. Monteverdi's *L'Orfeo* introduced another innovation, aside from his choice of the tragic conclusion. He treated the convention of *recitar cantando* more freely than the Florentines had done; he expanded monody so

that arias became lyric expressions with accompaniment, and he gave greater stature to the choruses. He composed for a larger, more richly varied and subtle orchestra, capable of wonderful tonal expression (the opening *toccata*), and his careful, dramatically apt instrumentation allowed for such variegated coloring as, for example, in the use of the chamber organ just at the moment when Orpheus glances back at Eurydice and loses her forever. The emotional style of the singing is mirrored in the vibrant, dense instrumental interludes or *sinfonie*, articulating and framing the plot. These often take the form of *ritornelli*, as when the somber tones of the wind instruments prepare for Orpheus's descent into the underworld, or the strings and flutes accompany his sorrowful return to the fields of Thrace. The opera ends with an apotheosis: Orpheus is carried to heaven by Apollo (no such scene appears in Poliziano's version), and the concluding ballet is a triumphant "Moresca."

Although Monteverdi's compositions are closely bound to the text, he allows his music in many places to break through the surface of the drama so that his heroes

Orpheus as a child: Ceiling decoration in the Camera degli sposi. This room for the betrothed, decorated with frescoes by Andrea Mantegna, is one of the main attractions of the Palazzo Ducale in Mantua. During Monteverdi's time, the palace itself, a kind of ensemble of different buildings with more than 500 rooms, housed the largest collection of art in Italy, including early paintings by Peter Paul Rubens, who had been court painter in Mantua. In 1627 the collection was sold to Charles I of England for financial reasons.

may express themselves by purely musical means. For example, they "speak" in daring interval leaps and dissonances and still more plainly in audacious ornamentation, the expression of violent emotion. The virtuosity of these embellishments and the repetition of long notes at the end of a phrase are the beginnings of the cadenzas of the later bravura arias and the model for that kind of "excited" instrumental style (*stile concitato*) that Monteverdi himself perfected in his cantata, *Il combattimento di Tancredi e Clorinda* (1624).

In 1613 Monteverdi became conductor and composer of the Cathedral of St. Mark in Venice and remained in this position until his death. Most of the great theatrical works of this time have been lost, among them, the comic opera *La finta pazza Licori* (1627). Two late works, however, have survived: *Il ritorno d'Ulisse in patria* (1640) and *L'incoronazione di Poppea* (1643). They continued the tradition of *L'Orfeo*, but stressed even more the importance of arias, duets, and ensembles. The form of the recitative grew freer and more flowing, without becoming musically inconsequential as the trite, hurried recitative of the newer style later on.

L'incoronazione di Poppea was one of the first operas not intended

L'Orfeo at the Salzburg Festspiele, 1993; stage production by Herbert Wernicke, conductor René Jacobs. Jacobs uses the tonal possibilities of a large intermedio orchestra. There are two *basso continuo* groups (organ, harpsichord, regal, theorbo), five string instruments and bass viol, and a third group (harp, lute, lyre, and two bass viols), cornets, flutes, dulciana, and percussion.

for the court but for a public opera house: the Teatro Santi Giovanni e Paolo in Venice. This explains why the orchestra is smaller than in *L'Orfeo*, and the composer even dispensed with the choruses.

The *Poppea* is a perfect example of an early Venetian opera; it is thought to have influenced future operas because of its clearly differentiated yet typical characters. *Poppea* offers us the noble lovers paired with a couple of a lower social station, the comical elderly woman and the servant in love, who lives on in Mozart's Cherubino (*Marriage of Figaro*) and Strauss's Octavian (*Der Rosenkavalier*).

There are a number of differences between the text of *L'Orfeo* that appeared in 1607 and the full score printed two years later. The libretto closely follows Poliziano's conclusion: Orpheus in his sorrow renounces all women and is pursued by the furious Bacchae, whose dance concludes the story. In the full-score version, Apollo leads Orpheus to heaven. Unlike the full score of *Euridice* (1600), the printed editions of *L'Orfeo* (1609, 1615) contain details about instrumentation. The fact that it was printed twice indicates the high regard in which this opera was held at the time.

The first century of opera:
The steps to success

It is unlikely today that people will soliloquize or communicate with each other by singing, least of all in poetry. It is unlikely that anyone ever did, at least not in "recent" historical memory. And yet, it is at least theoretically possible that once, in very distant times, gods, spirits, men or human-like creatures did communicate in song. The poets and composers who, at the turn of the 17th century, set out upon the adventure of writing operas brushed over the irrationality of their plots by setting the action in a fairy-tale landscape with the Greek mythological figure of Orpheus as the central character—Orpheus who, as a legend, personifies song. Likewise, Daphne, a nymph in the realm of Pan, the shepherd god, is the heroine of the first opera; she is a part of Orpheus's legendary realm. In fact, the opera composers of this time did not aspire toward any simple naturalism; they aimed at the illusion of reality (*verosimiglianza*), with the emphasis on illusion. And they legitimized their efforts historically on the basis of the declamatory style of the ancient Greek tragedies. Within another 50 years, opera had become an established form of art. Opera was opera; that operas were sung was obvious. Now the form could develop and evolve: Opera as a genre no longer needed to restrict itself to associations with myths and shepherds' plays. At the same time, another old convention was discarded; in fact, it was reversed: Whereas Monteverdi had subordinated the music to the word, or rather to the dramatic rhetoric ("L'oratione sia padrona dell'armonia e non serva"), his followers rather held to the dictum: music first and then the word! ("Prima la musica e poi le parole").

Venice: The first opera companies

The opera *L'Andromeda*, by Benedetto Ferrari and Francesco Manelli (both leaseholders in the theater) was performed in Venice in 1637 for the inauguration of the first public opera house, the Teatro San Cassiano. The music of this opera has not survived, but the libretto reworks a story from classical Greek mythology. Andromeda was the daughter of Cepheus and Cassiopeia, who aroused the wrath of Poseidon by claiming her daughter was fairer than the Nereids. Andromeda was to be sacrificed to a sea monster but was rescued by Perseus and became a constellation after her death.

With opera better established as an art form, legends like this were increasingly replaced by historical subjects. Monteverdi started the trend with *L'Incoronazione di Poppea*, which revolves around the historical figure of Nero, who sent

Perseus hurries through the air to free Andromeda, chained to a rock, from the sea monster. (Engraving by Francesco Guitti, 17th century.) The box above the stairs could represent a kind of orchestra pit.

23

Teatro Grimani a S.Geovanni Grisostomo

With the commercial success of opera in the Teatro San Cassiano, many new theaters suddenly cropped up. Within a few decades, six new theaters opened. In 1678, the Teatro Grimani opened; it was also known as the Teatro San Giovanni Crisostomo, after the neighboring church. Inside, five galleries rose one above the other to include 175 boxes, and, as the copper engraving shows, a twelve-member orchestra seemed sufficient for so large a house.

his wife Ottavia into exile so that he might make his mistress Poppea the empress. Monteverdi's opera retains some antiquarian features, such as the allegorical figures of Fortune, Virtue, and Love, who appear in the prologue.

Comic elements are a mainstay of early Venetian opera. Typical of the humor of this period is a delight in the escapades of rogues and servants. Such characters were plentiful in Spanish dramas and picaresque novels and from there made their way into librettos. They satisfied the appetite of the paying audience for good entertainment. The aristocrats, as owners, continued to have the final say in the theaters (by 1640, three theaters in Venice had been converted into opera houses, and not long after that seven houses were competing with each other), but the leaseholders determined what would be played and they tended to cater to the tastes of their audience. The audiences themselves consisted of people from all walks of life: the ordinary citizens in the round pit or courtyard, the more important people in the boxes that were rented out permanently.

The commercialization of opera and the growing number of productions prompted measures to simplify and economize even the musical forms. The variety in Monteverdi's works was gradually reduced to a rigid sequence of recitative and aria, with almost no support from choruses and ensembles. The aria itself was confined to a *da capo* form, the so-called intermediate aria (*mezz'aria*) was composed as an accompanied recitative, and the remnants of what was once the *recitar cantando* disappeared in the short *recitativo secco*. Even the orchestra shrank in size in comparison with the earlier *intermedio* orchestras of the courts.

Mistaken identity, confusion, and intrigue were usually at the heart of the fairly predictable, schematic plots of most librettos. Lighthearted comic scenes interrupted the central plot, which usually involved two pairs of lovers from different social circles and various minor characters, among which the comic servant was seldom missing.

Many of the librettists of the 17th century were merely occasional poets. Their pay often consisted only of the proceeds from the sale of the text. The practice of reading along in the text

La Fenice, the most famous and, with its 2,000 seats, also the largest opera house in Vienna, was built at the end of the 18th century, after its predecessor the Teatro San Benedetto had burned down. (Engraving by Domenico Cagnoni, 19th century.)

25

A view of San Marco, the domain of Claudio Monteverdi. Francesco Cavalli, a tenor in Monteverdi's chorus, became his pupil. Cavalli's *L'Ormindo* premiered in 1644 in the Teatro San Cassiano. It is one of 42 operas written by Cavalli, 28 of which have survived. Together with Monteverdi and Antonio Cesti, the younger, whose first opera, *L'Orontea*, was performed in Venice in 1649, Cavalli is the most important representative of the early Venetian opera, which grew to be equally popular outside Italy.

during the performance gave rise to a means of earning supplementary income—selling wax candles to opera patrons.

One of the best Venetian opera librettists was Gian Francesco Busenello, a lawyer by profession, who wrote five librettos, including *Poppea* for Monteverdi and *La Didone* for Francesco Cavalli. Often imitated, Giovanni Faustini was an equally fine librettist, who wrote dozens of opera texts, some of which were set to music by Cavalli. Neither Busenello nor Faustini, however, ever produced the sheer quantities achieved by Niccolò Minato and Apostolo Zeno. Each wrote more than fifty operas as well as many oratorio texts for the Viennese court.

L'incoronazione di Poppea in a production by Jürgen Flimm at the Salzburger Festspiele in 1993. (Scenery by Rolf Glittenberg; musical conductor and director Nikolaus Harnoncourt.)

Rome: Musical theater with the Church's blessing

Two works marked the beginning of Roman opera: *La rappresentazione di anima e di corpo*, by Emilio de' Cavalieri (1600), and the pastoral drama *Eumelio*, by Agostino Agazzari (1606). Although both works fall within the tradition of the ecclesiastical play or school drama, they also were stylistically closely related to Florentine operas, and as such helped generate interest in this new genre in Rome. But nearly twenty years would pass before the first real Roman operas were performed. Predictably, the first was another version of the Orpheus legend, *La morte d'Orfeo* by Stefano Landi (1619); the second, *L'Aretusa* by Filippo Vitali (1620), was a musical setting of a pastoral drama.

Landi may be considered the first who served as both composer and librettist for his works. His treatment of the figure of the drunken ferryman Caronte in his Orpheus opera is so markedly comic that it presages the 18th century schism of operas into the comic *opera buffa* and the more serious *opera seria*. Cardinal Antonio and Cardinal Francisco Barberini, both nephews of Pope Urban VIII, were the most important patrons of the Roman opera. They organized the performance of Stefano Landi's *Il Sant' Alessio* in 1632 in the newly built theater of the Palazzo Barberini,

Monica Bacelli as Diana and Maria Bayo in the title role of Cavalli's *La Calisto* in the 1993 production of Herbert Wernicke at the Théâtre Royal de La Monnaie in Brussels. René Jacobs, musical director.

which could accommodate an audience of 3,000. This was the first "religious" opera in history; it was also one of the first operas to begin with a *sinfonia* with several movements that functioned as a real overture ("per introduzione del prologo"). The title role called for a *castrato*; in the Church State, all high passages of vocal music and female roles were sung by men well into the 18th century. The ingenious scenery and staging devices were designed by the papal architect Gian Lorenzo Bernini. The libretto, replete with many comic scenes, was written by Cardinal Giulio Rospigliosi, who would later become Pope Clemens IX. A year later, Rospigliosi penned *Chi soffre, speri*, in which the comic servants sing partly in dialect; the influence of the Italian *commedia dell'arte* tradition is unmistakeable. The opera itself, with music by Virgilio Mazzocchi and Marco Marazzoli, is a forerunner of the later *opera buffa*. The feudal background of the Roman opera, the occasion for more luxury, more performers, more elaborate staging and scenery—more than was thus far known in Venetian productions—marked a pinnacle for the typical Roman penchant for choruses and spectacular mechanical effects.

The early flowering of Roman opera came to a sudden and drastic end under Pope Innocent X,

The most important patrons of the Roman opera and of the oratorio were members of the pope's family. Palaces like the Palazzo Pamphili, which belonged to the nobility, housed theater halls.

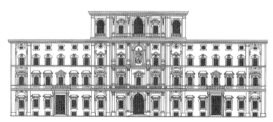

who drove the Barberini clan out of the city. The new pope preferred religious oratorios. Many artists and composers chose to follow the Barberini to France where they had gone to seek asylum. Among them was Luigi Rossi, whose tragicomedy per musica *Orfeo* premiered in the theater hall of the Louvre during the carnival season of 1647. This work made many concessions to current French fashions in its interspersed ensembles, its ballets, and interludes written for full orchestra. But its success was not enduring. Only the frequent time shifts, a hallmark of Rossi's work, would remain a stylistic element used in later French operas.

Paris: Opera and ballet at the court of Louis XIV

Neither Roman operas nor the commercially successful Venetian operas held any special place or value for the ballet. In France, where the *tragédie en musique* developed in the last third of the 17th century, the situation was quite different. The "inventors" of this singular type of opera, later called *tragédie lyrique*, were Jean-Baptiste Lully, the Italian court composer of Louis XIV, and his librettist Philippe Quinault, whose polished verses (written mainly in alexandrine rhythm) emphasized the high artistic level of this new form. Together, over a period of 15 years, the two collaborated on a good dozen operas, most of which were mythological in subject matter. The works by Lully and Quinault were considered the model of opera for nearly 100 years and were widely admired even outside their native France.

In both Paris and Versailles, Lully had a superb orchestra at his disposal. In addition, institutions such as the school of ballet and the *Académie Royale de Musique* (an opera academy with something of a monopoly over opera training) finally enabled the French to counteract the influx of Italian operas such as Cavalli's *Serse* (Xerxes, 1660), which were both un-popular and expensive to import. Now, instead, the French could present their own operas, which Lully tried for the first time in 1662. He refashioned Cavalli's *L'Ercole amante*. Cavalli had tried to adapt his opera to French taste himself by adding many choruses. Lully, on the other hand, composed some new ballets that turned out to be more popular than the opera itself. After *Psyché* (1671), which could be considered a last trial run, Lully wrote *Cadmus et Hermione* (1673), which was the first completely accomplished *tragédie en musique*. Thereafter, Lully produced a new opera almost every year. *Alceste* (1674) was followed by *Atys* (1676), then followed works like *Phaéton* (1683) and *Armide et Renaud* (1686). He died in 1687, from an injury he sustained while conducting his *Te Deum* for the convalescing king. Lully was wounded in the foot with the point of a long *baton* he was using to beat time and the injury turned gangrenous and proved fatal.

Jean-Baptiste Lully, born in Italy, worked his way up to become the ruler of France's musical circles under Louis XIV. The stages of his ascent: garçon de chambre, language teacher, dancer, actor, and finally composer.

In its tightly woven dramatic structure, the *tragédie lyrique*, consisting of five acts and a prologue, is closely related to the three-act Italian operas. Yet the choice of subject matter, the spectacular *deus-ex-machina* effects, the sumptuous scenery and staging, and especially the ostentatious homage to the ruler during the prologue render these works reminiscent

A ballet scene from Lully's last opera *Armide et Renaud* (1686), based on episodes from the epic poem, *Gerusalemme liberata*, by Torquato Tasso. The sorceress Armida loses her magical powers because of her love for the crusader Rinaldo. She tries to kill Rinaldo while he is sleeping. This is one of the most famous "slumber scenes" in all operatic literature, and even Johann Sebastian Bach drew on the music in a chorus of his *St. Matthew Passion*.

of the festive *intermedii* of earlier times. They also bear a strong resemblance to the *ballet de cour*, a genre to which Lully contributed, too, and that continued to be fashionable in France. Like the *opéra-ballet*, which lacks a unifying plot, or the *comédie-ballet*, which combines dance and drama (most notably those written by the great French comic playwright Molière), these grand ballets are comparable to the *tragédie lyrique* in their brilliance but they are looser and less unified in form. In fact, they do not aspire to the same artistic level: The *tragédie lyrique*, unlike these other forms, strives to embody a unified artistic concept; it is what is known in German as a "*Gesamtkunstwerk.*"

Cavalli's *L'Ercole amante* was performed in 1662 for the inauguration of the Salle des Machines in the Tuileries, which had been remodeled as a theater hall. Lully composed the music for the ballets.

Like the many choruses and the extended dance and song *divertissements*, the orchestra overture, framing the prologue, is

31

also an obligatory part of the *tragédie lyrique*. The overture usually has a three-part form (slow-quick-slow) with a weighty beginning in a precisely punctuated rhythm, followed by a central *fugato*, a structure that became a model for many different kinds of instrumental music throughout Europe. The purely instrumental part of the *tragédie lyrique* is much longer than that of Italian operas. With the short pieces linking scenes, the tonal compositions depicting storms or other events, the *entr'actes*, and the attendant ballets, performances of a *tragédie lyrique* could last more than four hours.

Since Lully, the lengthy *chaconne*, usually placed at the close of an act, has been a constituent element in the inventory of an opéra-ballet as well as of a *tragédie lyrique*.

The French Baroque opera also differs from the Italian in the importance given to recitative and aria. The French *récitatif* is rich in nuance and stays close to the high level of the poetry; its Italian counterpart by the end of the century tended toward casual recitative, musically almost a stereotype in its cliché-ridden formulas. The Italian

The destruction of Armida's palace in Lully's opera required some ingenious staging mechanics. (Draft of an engraving by the theater architect Jean Berain.)

arias, on the other hand, developed into the main attraction of the opera. Sweeping, musically coherent, and artfully constructed strophic works, they demand a singer with excellent technique and dramatic virtuosity. The French airs remain more song-like, dependent on the verse form and on the so-called natural pattern of speech. To Italian ears, the difference between recitative and aria in French works was barely discernible, according to an anecdote about the poet Carlo Goldoni.

The privileged position that Lully enjoyed at the court of the Louis XIV inevitably influenced the style of his successors. Nevertheless, both Marc-Antoine Charpentier, who published no operas during the life of his dominant competitor, as well as the younger André Campra, brought distinct innovations to the genre of the *tragédie lyrique*.

Both Charpentier and Campra tried carefully to close the rift between French and Italian opera. A great example of this attempt at synthesis is *Les fêtes vénitiennes* (1710), in which Campra depicted and finally reconciled the rivalry between the differing national styles with great elegance and humor. Of course, the rivalry between Italian and French opera continued, taking the form of an ongoing debate over the predominance of Italian music over French, which started in the middle of the 17th century and continued in artistic circles. The controversy finally came to a head 100 years later in the *Querelle des Bouffons*, which pitted *tragédie lyrique* against *opera buffa*. Ultimately, this ushered in the end of the *tragédie lyrique* as it was known, though it would reemerge in all its classical splendor in the late works of Jean-Philippe Rameau; the texts of the later *tragédies lyriques*, however, would never quite match the artistic excellence attained earlier by Quinault.

Naples: Europe's opera training ground

The rapid spread of Venetian opera throughout Italy was in part due to traveling groups of performers such as the "Febi armonici," who were originally members of professional acting companies. While the Roman opera wielded a great influence over the court opera in France, Venetian operas had a direct impact on the course of opera in Naples, where, at the turn of the 18th century, opera began to be mass-produced.

Francesco Provenzale is considered the first Neapolitan opera composer. In 1673 Provenzale became head of the *Conservatorio della Pietà dei Turchini*, an orphanage, which through its systematic musical education turned out to be the leading training ground for fine musicians. Only two of Provenzale's operas survive, *Il schiavo di sua moglie* (1672) and *La Stellidaura vendicante* (1674). The latter is a turbulent drama of jealousy and intrigue, featuring the role of a dialect-speaking, comic servant.

Next to Provenzale, the Venetian Pietro Andrea Ziani was the most successful opera composer in Naples. Ziani had taught at the *Conservatorio San Onofrio* from 1678 and served as composer and conductor to the viceroy from 1680. His successor in this position in

1684 was Alessandro Scarlatti, who was educated in Rome. Scarlatti was to write more than 100 operas, about a third of which have survived. His greatest success in Naples was the comic opera, *Il trionfo dell'onore*, performed more than eighteen times after the premiere. Despite his success, however, Scarlatti is not regarded as the main exponent of the Neapolitan school, which would decidedly influence the structural development of 18th century opera.

In his early works in particular, Scarlatti is clearly in the Venetian tradition, with its comparatively colorful recitative and its wealth of aria forms. But he faithfully followed one of the most prominent conventions of Neapolitan opera, the three-part symphony (fast-slow-fast) as overture. It is in his later operas that one will hear *da capo* arias accompanied by the orchestra as well as the *accompagnato* (recitative with orchestral rather than *basso continuo* accompaniment).

"Throat of Hell": scene by Ludovico Burnacini from Antonio Cesti's *Il Pomo d'oro*. Charon, the ferryman of the underworld, is crossing the river of Hell; in the background a city burns. This opera was performed in 1668 for the opening of the imperial opera house in the Cortina in Vienna. The opera house was designed by Burnacini; unfortunately, this enormous building (213 feet long, 88 feet wide, and 49 feet high) was destroyed by Turkish troops in 1683.

Carlo Broschi, also known as Farinelli, was the most famous of the castrati. He had his debut in Vienna in 1724. After unparalleled success as the star of the London "Opera of the Nobility" under Nicola Porpora, he went to Madrid in 1737. Here he was director of the opera until 1760 and became the confidential friend of Spanish kings.

The Baroque opera outside Italy and France

The foreign powers that reigned in Italy for hundreds of years managed to have no negative influence on the history of the opera, which is essentially an Italian phenomenon. Indeed, the various relations to Austria, Spain, and France simply made it easier for Italian operas to be exported abroad. The French *tragédie lyrique* could hardly stave off the almost suffocating dominance of Italian operas in the 17th and 18th centuries.

The imperial court in Vienna was the largest "importer" of Italian operas, and with them the necessary musicians and technicians. Venetian opera set the tone; it was represented through such composers as Antonio Cesti, Pietro Andrea Ziani, and Antonio Draghi. The latter wrote well over 100 operas, mostly with librettos taken from the work of Niccolò Minato, who was appointed court poet in 1669. An artistic highpoint of Draghi's work during his tenure as imperial "Intendant der Theatermusik" (from 1673) and court composer and conductor (from 1682) were the *rappresentazioni sacre* or *azioni sacre*. These are religious musical dramas that were performed in Vienna during Lent and times of fasting when the opera and theaters remained closed. From the time of Ferdinand III, this genre was held in high esteem by the royal family.

Leopold I was himself the composer of several oratorios and *azioni sacre*. Within this tradition, a special performance niche was reserved for the *sepolcri*, which deal with the burial of Christ and were presented only during the Holy Week. This tradition continued until the reign of Charles VI in the 18th century, at which time the scenic *rappresentazioni* and the *sepolcri* were replaced by oratorio concerts.

The most important operatic occasion in Vienna was the premiere of Antonio Cesti's *Il Pomo d'oro*, with text by Francesco Sbarra. This opera was written to celebrate the marriage of Leopold I to the Spanish *infanta* Margaret. It tells of the judgment of the Trojan prince Paris, who was asked to decide which goddess—Venus, Athena, or Juno—is the most beautiful. Paris finally awards the golden apple, Discordia, to Venus. Athena and Juno then try to destroy Paris, until Jupiter, tired of the fighting, steals the apple and gives it, as a symbol of the unity of the empire, to Margaret, the new empress. The architect and set designer Ludovico Ottavio Burnacini designed twenty-four different settings for this mammoth production, consisting of a prologue and five acts, with a total of sixty-seven scenes. The performance lasted over ten hours and was split over two afternoons. Nearly fifty different singers were required for the roles. Johann Heinrich Schmelzer, who would later become court composer, composed the music for the many ballet numbers. While this spectacle was one of the costliest ever produced, only an incomplete version of the score has survived; the music for the third and fifth acts has been lost.

Farinelli in the role of a woman (caricature by Pierleone Ghezzi, Rome, 1724).

Because such gala opera productions were exorbitantly costly, with their demands for an enormous number of people and excessive outlays for scenery and costumes and the like, they remained the exception, rather than the rule, even in Vienna. Most Viennese operas, like the Venetian productions, consisted of three acts, half a dozen central singing roles, and singers in minor roles singing more than one part. Many of the main male roles were intended for altos or sopranos, ranges today sung by women though sometimes also by falsettos or countertenors. During the Baroque period, these roles were sung by castrati, such as Ferri, Senesino, Farinelli and Cafarelli, the celebrated stars of Italian opera.

The Italian influence eventually extended well beyond Austria. It can be heard, for example, in the music of Spain, which, with Naples, Sicily, and Sardinia, ruled the greatest part of Italy until the start of the War of Succession (1701–1713/14). Italian opera finally had a breakthrough in Spain only in the 18th century. Until then, Spain enjoyed its own independent tradition of music theater called the *zarzuela*. The *zarzuela* grew out of three-act Spanish dramas whose only musical component came in the form of musical interludes. The two forms later merged into a dramatically unified two-act structure. The retention of spoken dialogue perpetuated the ties to drama. The first production of a South American opera took place in 1701 at the court of the viceroy in Lima, Peru: This was *La púrpura de la rosa*, by Tomás de Torrejón y Velasco.

In England, in the mid-17th century, the Italian influence was at first hindered by civil war and the ban on theaters under the protectorate of Oliver Cromwell. In the second half of the century, the English music theater took its first tentative steps toward Italian opera and toward the *tragédie lyrique*, then still in the process of development. The English tradition, however, was more strongly affected by the native English masque than by any continental imports. Early English operas were, more than those of any other operatic tradition thus far, made up of choruses and

The castrati are so accustomed to female roles that the best actresses in the world could not perform better. Their voices are just as soft, but stronger, and they tend to be taller than the average woman and so have more majesty. ... Ferini, for example, who played the role of Sibari in the opera *Temistocle* in Rome in 1698, is larger and more beautiful than women ... clothed as the Persian princess, with turban and aigrette, he had the look of a queen and empress; and perhaps no one has ever seen a more beautiful woman than he seemed in this costume.

Abbé François Raguenet on the castrati (in: Parallèle des Italiens et des François en ce qui regarde la musique et les opéras, 1702)

dances. Henry Purcell's *Dido and Aeneas*, written in 1689, of all the earliest English operas, perhaps comes closest to the conventional form. *Dido* is a three-act opera with a French overture and prologue, but still runs no longer than an hour. In later works such as *King Arthur* (1691) or *The Fairy Queen* (1693), Purcell returned to a sort of semi-opera (with spoken dialogue), thereby placing himself firmly in the path worn by his predecessors, most notably Matthew Locke, who wrote *Psyche* in 1675.

Although Italian musicians could be found at the court in Dresden from the middle of the 16th century, the first performance of an Italian opera did not take place until 1662: *Il Paride*, by Giovanni Andrea Bontempi. In 1671 in the Taschenberg opera house, which had been completed just four years before, Bontempi's *Teutsche musicalische Opera von der Daphne* was performed; in subject, it revives the lost opera of Heinrich Schütz from 1627.

Gentile Borgondio, here shown in women's clothing, was, with Girolamo Crescentini (the famous imperial singing teacher in Vienna and Paris), one of the last great castrati. He ended his career in 1812. In the papal Sistine Chapel, where women's voices were not allowed, castrati still sang into the beginning of the 20th century.

In 1716, a year after he was appointed court conductor in Vienna, Johann Joseph Fux composed the opera *Angelica, Vincitrice di Alcina*, on the occasion of the birth of the prince. Giuseppe Galli-Bibiena, the most famous theater architect of his time, designed the costumes and settings. The open-air staging took place in the garden of the *Favorita* by night in a so-called pool-theater— a stage built around a pond on which ships and artificial islands appear.

Helga Schmidt as Errea in Agostino Steffani's heroic-comic drama *Enrico Leone* (with a libretto by Ortensio Mauro), newly performed in Hannover, Germany, in 1989 (production and staging by Herbert Wernicke; musical director, Lajos Rovatkay). Two hundred years earlier, this work had been performed for the opening of the first opera house in Hannover, a building with about 1,300 seats and with ingenious technical staging devices: "A ship which breaks apart. A griffin that leads Heinrich to its nest. A battle between a griffin and a lion. The appearance, through magic, of Heinrich in the ante-chamber of Metilda. A cloud that brings Heinrich to the Kalkberg near Lüneburg. A devil who throws a lion into the air. The siege and conquest of Bardewick. A triumphal chariot drawn by four live horses."

Munich also enjoyed lively contact with Italy, and it was here, in 1658, that an old granary was refurbished as an opera house—the "Salvatortheater." Unfortunately, none of the operas by Johann Kaspar Kerll, known to have been performed there, have survived. In 1681, Agostino Steffani was appointed director of chamber music at the electoral court. Until he left for Hannover in 1688, Steffani composed five operas for Munich, most of which are at least partially lost. For the opening of the new palace theater in Hannover in 1689, Steffani composed *Enrico Leone*, an Italian opera with a French overture—this was typical of Steffani's

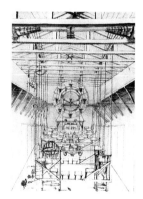

Elaborate machinery is hidden behind the movable cloud scenery in *Germanico sul Reno* by Giovanni Legrenzi (Venice, 1675, libretto by Giulio Cesare Corradi).

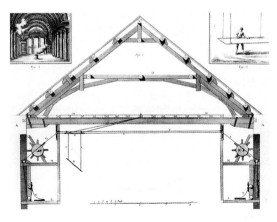

A flying device for Mercury who is floating down on a cloud, depicted in the *Encyclopédie* by Denis Diderot and Jean Le Rond d'Alembert (Paris, 1772).

work. *Enrico Leone* was played in various places, including in 1716 in Braunschweig in a German version by Georg Caspar Schürmann. Since the city hall on the Hagenmarkt was rebuilt as a theater in 1690, the German city of Braunschweig has continuously cultivated the opera tradition. Unlike the development in other German royal seats or capitals, Hamburg experienced a kind of bourgeois opera tradition that flowered from 1678 to 1738. Under the auspices of Reinhard Keiser, beginning in 1695 with the performance of his Braunschweig opera, *Der königliche Schäfer oder Basilius in Arcadien*, the opera in Hamburg began, in aesthetic terms, its most fruitful period.

Ever more and new flying devices, equipment and vehicles of all sorts and forms were demanded in order to convey the creatures of the air and everything that wants either to descend from heaven or to ascend from the abyss. And in operas there are many such strange beings to be expedited. The theater is often transformed twenty times during a single opera. No one is interested in the decorum of the scenery. Cities, houses, mountains and forests, illuminated halls filled with statues, courtyards and bedrooms follow upon each other, back and forth, up and down. Triumphal carriages, litters, riders with horses, camels, and boats, drive, gallop, and push each other back and forth. Each new opera needs new clothes, without real jewels of course, but all the more expensive because of the variety required.

Johann Friedrich Schütze on the Gänsemarkt-Oper
(Hamburgische Theatergeschichte [*The History of the Hamburg Theater*], 1794)

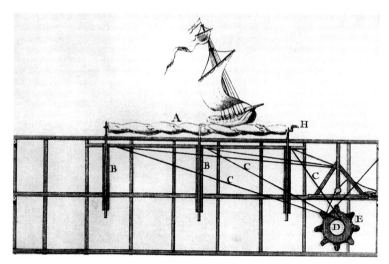

Constructions for ship and wave movements on the stage (*Encyclopédie*, Paris, 1772).

About 40 years after the founding of the first public opera houses in Venice, the *Oper am Gänsemarkt* (at the geese market) was opened in Hamburg in 1678. This theater was to operate solely on a commercial basis; admission was open to anyone who paid the entrance fee. The owners, as well as the members of the board of directors, were wealthy citizens, among them the organist Johann Adam Reinken. Ambitious composers such as Johann Theile were eager to leave their mark on the new genre; Theile's opera *Der erschaffene, gefallene und auffgerichtete Mensch* was chosen to inaugurate the new opera house on the *Gänsemarkt*. Artistically minded men like the lawyers Christian Hinrich Postel and Barthold Feind, as well as the mayor of the city, Lucas von Bostel, wrote librettos as a hobby.

Since staging techniques were already quite advanced in northern Germany, mechanical effects and the possibilities for scene transformations in Hamburg were as good as any found in court theaters. From 1695 to 1702, Johann Oswald Harms, a native of Hamburg, was responsible for the decor and costumes. Having spent many years of training and education in Italy, Harms worked at the opera houses in Dresden and Braunschweig. He became one of the leading scene painters of his time and created the sets to Keiser's opera *Störtebeker* (1701). This opera is one of the many lost works of a repertoire of over 250 operas. (A considerable portion of the losses was due to the Second World War.)

Reinhard Keiser was not the most prominent man who worked for the Hamburg opera house; the young Georg Friedrich Handel and the older Georg Philipp Telemann were both actively employed here. Keiser, however, was leaseholder of the opera house from 1703 to 1707 and, as such, directed its course. He was also its most prolific supplier: Keiser composed more than eighty operas for Hamburg in thirty years. The range of titles of his operas—such as *Basilius, Störtebeker*, and *Croesus* (1711, revised version 1730)—show that the subject matter of these operas was in no way prescribed, unlike the opera tradition already established in France. Perhaps that is why these operas were examined with such a critical eye by both clerical and civil authorities.

"Tempest on the stage," by Johann Oswald Harms, probably for the German version of Steffani's *Enrico Leone*, performed in Hamburg in 1696.

The heroes of Baroque operas wore plumes and trains, in addition to a mid-calf-length costume reminiscent of Roman coats of mail, usually sewn like a hoop skirt ("tonnelet").

Through the colorful diversity of its comic subplots and minor characters, and through the mixture of German, a northern German dialect, Italian, and French songs, the Hamburg operas fell prey to a development that had already been successfully curbed in Italy. There, librettists such as Apostolo Zeno and Pietro Metastasio, had radically weeded out the equally rank growth in Venetian operas. The upshot of this reform process was the exclusion of comic elements, thereby reducing the number of actors and tightening the plot. Unfortunately, the price paid for this reform was a growing schematization that became the dominant characteristic of Italian operas in the 18th century.

In the face of various accusations of immorality, the opera house was closed a number of times during its early years. In 1688, a commission from Jena University was given the authority once and for all to decide whether it was sinful to watch or perform such musical works. In 1725, the opera house was closed again because of the performance of Keiser's opera *Die Hamburger Schlachtzeit*, a local farce considered by a contemporary as an affront to scenery, music, and even the nation itself.

Hamburg's first opera, composed by Johann Theile.

Der erschaffene/ gefallene und auffgerichtete Mensch.

In einem Singe-Spiel vorgestellet.

Inhalt und Vor-Bericht.

Cœsus/ ein so hochmüthiger/ als reicher König in Lidien/ dem Griechischen Philosopho Solon/ dem er seine Schätze zeigete/ und seine Glück-seligkeit rühmete/ nicht glauben wollend/ daß vor dem Tode kein Mensch sich glücklich nennen möge/ muste nachmahls die Wahrheit selbigen Ausspruchs in der That erfahren/ und mit seinem eigenen Bey-spiel erweisen/ daß/ wer am höchsten sitzet/ am tieffe-sten fallen könne. Er hatte die von denen Assyriern/ wider ihren Landes-Herrn Cirus/ erregte Rebellion/ nicht allein heimlich befördert/ sondern auch öffentlich mit seinen Krieges-Schaaren gestärcket/ und den da-durch beleidigten Persischen Monarchen so sehr erzür-net/ daß derselbe/ sich zu rächen/ mit einem Krieges-Heer ihn überzog/ die Liedier in der ersten Feld-Schlacht aufs Haupt erlegte/ und den König selbst ge-fangen nahm/ nachdem dessen vorhin stummer Sohn Atis, durch Krafft des natürlichen Triebes und kindli-cher Liebe/ in der/ dem Herrn Vater obschwebenden höchsten Lebens Gefahr/ die Bande der Zungen zerris-sen/ mit denen Worten: **Halt! erschlag den König nicht/** eines feindlichen Soldaten mörd-lichen Hieb gehemmet/ und ihn dadurch dem augen-scheinlichen Tode entrissen hatte.

Der Siegreiche Perser war mit dieser Rache nicht vergnüget/ verdammete den gefangenen König zum Feuer/ und konte durch den Himmel selbst/ der mit star-ckem Platz-Regen/ als mittleidigen Thränen/ die Flammen dämpffete/ nicht besänfftiget werden/ Wie aber zuletzt der Hülff- und Hoffnung-lose Cœsus in der Gluth der von ihm vormahls verspotteten des Welt-Weisen Lehre eingedenck/ in die Worte: O Solon, So-lon! mit lautem Geschrey ausbrach/ und Cirus sich de-ren Bedeutung erklären liesse/ schlug er in sich/ be-trachtete die Macht der Schickung/ die Unbeständig-keit des irdischen Glückes/ und die auch ihm dahero be-sorgende Gefahr; Befahl demnach, Cœsus vom Schei-ter-Hauffen abzuführen/ setzte ihn wieder in sein Reich/ und vorige Hoheit/ und verwandelte seinen Haß in eine beständige Freundschafft und nahe Verbündnisse.

Die Music zu dieser Opera, ist von des Herrn Capellmeister Keisers Composition.

Opera summary: a contem-porary "preview" of Reinhard Keiser's *Croesus*.

45

1701–1714
Spanish War of Succession.
1723
Johann Sebastian Bach works as Thomaskantor in Leipzig.
1735
William Hogarth paints *The Rake's Progress.*
1740
Friedrich II becomes King of Prussia.
1740–1748
Austrian War of Succession.
1751–1780
Denis Diderot and Jean Le Rond d'Alembert publish their *Encyclopédie*, which becomes one of the hallmarks of the Enlightenment.
1762
Catherine the Great becomes tsarina in Russia.

Celimene (Isabelle Poulenard) between her lovers, the poet Trigeno (Dominique Visse) and the boastful Filindo (Ralf Popken), in Caldara's opera *I Disingannati*, directed by Philippe Lénaël in Innsbruck, 1993 (musical director Sigiswald Kuijken). The Venetian Antonio Caldara, assistant court composer and conductor in Vienna with Johann Joseph Fux, was highly esteemed by the emperor for his religious oratorios.

Between absolutism and revolution:
From reform to reform

The age of the *basso continuo*, beginning with a change in style around 1600 and the cultivation of monody, slowly drew to an end in the 18th century. The practice of writing sequences of chords only through the notation of bass notes and some figures was discontinued in the full scores of operas. Completely composed orchestral instrumentation gained in importance, and the older practice was retained only in the *recitativo secco*. The reasons for this lay, in part, in the exemplary *tragédie lyrique*, which traditionally emphasized lengthy instrumental movements played by a full orchestra. The Italian opera also, however, began to evolve away from the *dramma musicale* to a kind of aria concert. As the characters of operas became more stereotypical and the plots less varied, essentially reduced to an inflexible schema, the need for a new, enriched operatic language became pressing.

It was not only the melodies of the songs with their expressive ornamentation but the orchestral instrumentation as well that became a vehicle for expressing deep emotion; this was already the case in the operas of Monteverdi, at least in a rudimentary form. In contrast to the 17th century operas, in which orchestras were assembled around the large group of *basso continuo* instruments, the heart of the 18th-century orchestras was the string family. By the end of the century, *basso continuo* instruments, particularly the bass lute, had almost completely disappeared. Only the harpsichord was retained as the indispensable instrument from which one could conduct or accompany the recitative, when the *accompagnato* was not already composed for instruments.

Metastasio and the *opera seria*

At the beginning of the 18th century, the Italian opera was still, to be blunt, muddled and confused. In efforts to please all the people all the time, the

1765
Joseph II assumes the throne of Austria.
1773
Boston Tea Party.
1789
Storming of the Bastille marks the beginning of the French Revolution.
1792
Ludwig van Beethoven studies with Joseph Haydn in Vienna ("Mozart's spirit from Haydn's hands").
1794
Condemnation and execution of Danton.
1799
Napoleon becomes First Consul.

Pietro Metastasio (actually P. Trapassi) was appointed imperial court poet in Vienna in 1730, succeeding Apostolo Zeno.

Johann Adolf Hasse, conductor and composer in Venice, Naples, and Dresden, set almost all of Metastasio's librettos to music.

entangled plots of dramatic intrigues, overburdened with comic elements, swung back and forth between farce and pathos. Understandably, the demand for reform did not arise from the audiences (although they would have had sufficient cause to complain about the irrationality of the operatic plots); it came, rather, from the literary critics who decried the scant artistic merits of the librettos.

A man of letters, Apostolo Zeno, who was called to Vienna to become court poet and historian in 1718, tried to elevate the value of librettos by modeling his texts on classical French drama, minimizing any comic or extraneous elements.

The Roman Pietro Metastasio, his successor as imperial court poet (*poeta cesareo*) took the reform of opera still further. In the hands of Metastasio's outstanding poetic talent, the libretto was freed from comic subplots, gods, and allegorical figures. The new opera texts not only managed to assert themselves against the old, they even became the basis for the success of the *opera seria*, which would dominate European musical life through the end of the century.

Metastasio's *drammi per musica* are equally effective without music. The bouncy rhythm of the verse and the ingenuity with which the author maneuvers his characters into seemingly hopeless crises or intrigues, only to get them out through a surprising but dramatically credible turn of events, unite his characters in a happy ending (*lieto fine*). Even if the basic situation of the six, or at most eight, characters remains unchanged, they nevertheless undergo a journey of purification, which allows their love and virtues to shine in a new light. While the basic ingredients of Metastasian aesthetics—the ancient ruler, the noble couple, honor and love—may no longer be palatable to the modern audience without the music, these very poetic qualities have inspired composers to their highest achievements. Especially significant in this context is the parabel metaphor, a formative principle in language often used by Metastasio in his texts and employed equally as a stimulus for coloristic tone-painting (*simile aria*).

Formally, the basic unit of Metastasio's librettos, like those of his successors, is a scene made up of a recitative followed by an exit aria. This structural principle had already been used by Zeno. Duets and ensembles, if any, have only a subordinate position in this design; a chorus is usually placed only at the end. Arias, following one another, become a kind of "hit parade," contrasting with each other through the changing emotions conveyed (love, despair, anger), and equally subject to internal contrasts. The arias usually had a two-verse structure, reflected in a change in mood between the A and B parts, between light and dark (*chiaroscuro*), a popular form of contrast in Baroque painting.

The most common types of the *Da capo* aria, which at this time usually has five parts (aa'-b-aa') articulated through short *ritornelli*, are as follows: the *aria di bravura* with rich *coloratura*, the *aria cantabile* with a melodious vocal part

Faustina Bordoni, one of the most celebrated prima donnas of her time, married Johann Adolf Hasse in 1730. Through their combined efforts, Dresden became a stronghold of Italian opera.

and simple accompaniment, the passionate *aria di mezzo carattere* with an emotional orchestral accompaniment, the *aria concertata* with the "concertizing" use of instruments, and finally the *aria parlante*, reserved for strong outbursts of emotion. The *aria di sorbetto* sung by a *seconda donna* or a *secondo uomo* remains an exception; this was the audience's opportunity to get refreshments and take a break.

Typical for the cult surrounding singers during the 18th century was the so-called suitcase aria (*aria di baule*), which had no connection with the plot. Interpolated at a suitable moment, this aria was a kind of "crowd pleaser," a chance for the star to display his or her virtuosity to its greatest advantage.

The continual repetition of basic types and emotions meant that arias were fundamentally interchangeable and could be used in a number of ways. At one extreme, when lack of money or time dictated, arias from different works could be strung together in "*pasticcio*" to form a "new" opera. For the performers, this practice offered a kind of pleasure in the repetitiveness, as each performance left the artist considerable room to expand his personal taste and his own style of ornamentation. The beautiful song (*bel canto*) became an artistic challenge, prompting the singer toward ever new and greater achievements: to extremely high notes, to breakneck interval leaps and scale runs, to smooth, lithe trills.

Metastasio's first libretto, *Didone abbandonata* (Naples, 1724) was set to music by Domenico

Antonio Vivaldi, called by his contemporaries "the red priest" (*prete rosso*) because of his clerical profession and his red hair, was an accomplished violinist and is known for composing hundreds of concertos for different instruments. He also composed about 50 operas. (Drawing by Pierleone Ghezzi, Rome 1723)

Sarro. It was a spectacular success, but it did come up against some heavy criticism because of its tragic conclusion. Nearly all of Metastasio's later opera dramas have a happy ending. He wrote a total of 27 operas, 20 of which are dated after 1730, the year in which he was summoned to the Habsburg Court in Vienna. His librettos were set to music, roughly speaking, about a thousand times, which earns Metastasio the honor of being the librettist most often set to music of all time. There are about forty musical versions of his *L'Olimpiade*, written in 1733 at the height of his career. Among these were scores by Antonio Caldara

In 1787, Mozart's contemporary Domenico Cimarosa went to St. Petersburg as conductor and composer for the tsar. In 1792, *Il matrimonio segreto* (The Secret Marriage, text by Giovanni Bertati) was produced. It was commissioned by the Austrian emperor; after its premiere he commanded that the opera be replayed that very evening. Shortly afterwards, this opera was performed on countless stages.

At the age of 21, Giovanni Battista Pergolesi was received commission (*scrittura*) to write his first opera: *Salustia* (Naples, 1732, libretto based on Apostolo Zeno). *La serva padrona*, written in 1733 and circulated throughout Europe by itinerant opera companies, became one of the most popular works of the 18th century. The caricature by Pierleone Ghezzi shows Pergolesi's handicap.

At the Prussian court, Friedrich II, who did not care for *Da capo* arias, initiated a very personal opera reform that was evident in the libretto he wrote himself: *Montezuma* (1755, Italian version by Giampetro Tagliazucchi). Although not entirely free of hypocrisy when we consider the Prussian wars of conquest in Europe, this opera was written under the spirit of

Enlightenment. The Christian *conquistadores* under Cortés are depicted as a barbarian horde, morally inferior to the Aztecs. Carl Heinrich Graun, who wrote the music to the exotic plot, composed only two arias in the usual style. Instead, he composed a number of two-part *cavatinas*, with and without orchestral preludes that lighten the dramatic structure. The climax is the concluding ballet scene that depicts Spanish atrocities against the background of the burning city. As one of the few *opera serias* with a tragic ending, *Montezuma* takes its place with Metastasio's *Didone abbandonata* in the "*film noir* aesthetic of the enlightened opera theater" (Karl Böhmer). Gasparo Spontini casts a positive light on the conquering of Mexico in *Fernand Cortez* (Paris 1809, text by Joseph Alphonse Esmérnard and Victor Joseph Etienne de Jouy) by having Cortez marry a Mexican woman. In Wolfgang Rihm's opera, *Die Eroberung von Mexiko* (The Emperor of Mexico, Hamburg, 1981, text after Antonin Artaud), the confrontation of two cultures is depicted as a sexual battle: Montezuma, seen as female, defends the "feminine" world against the "masculine" one of the Spanish conqueror.

(1733), Antonio Vivaldi (1734), Giovanni Battista Pergolesi (1735), and Leonardo Leo (1737); decades later, versions were produced by composers such as Johann Adolf Hasse (1756) and Domenico Cimarosa (1784). The popularity of his works proves that Metastasio's aristocratic dramas not only were appreciated by the nobility but were considered by many the ideal expression of his time.

Intermezzo and opera buffa

Zeno and Metastasio had successfully cleared the debris out of librettos, but this did not signify the extinction of comic figures and action on the opera stage. Instead, a new genre arose, the *opera buffa*, which spread from Italy throughout the rest of Europe just as quickly as the *opera seria* had done.

It is difficult to pinpoint a precise moment at which the 18th-century Italian opera split into a serious and a cheerful genre. One decisive factor was the practice of ending the acts of serious operas with a *scena buffa* or an *intermezzo*. In both Venice and Naples this convention was common: in 1733 in Naples, Pergolesi wrote his two-part *La serva padrona*, which was to become the most famous of all intermezzi (with text by Gennaro Antonio Federico). Originally intended for the close of the first and second acts of Pergolesi's opera, *Il prigioniero superbo*, it was soon performed elsewhere (even as an interlude in Hasse's *Demetrio* in Dresden, 1740). Comedies with music (*cummedeja pe'mmuseca*) were another Neapolitan specialty; these were not readily

Niccolò Jommelli attained success as court composer and conductor in Stuttgart with his highly French influenced opera *Fetonte* (first version 1753, second version 1768, text by Mattia Verazi). It is an opera seria with "program music," choruses, and ballets, emotional accompagnati and ensembles woven into complex scenes. The final tableau is impressive, importing techniques from the buffa finale to the large apparatus of the court opera.

Venetian playwright Carlo Goldoni was the most successful dramatist of his time. He wrote 69 buffo librettos, although, even in his own estimation, they could not compete with his timeless comedies, such as *Mirandolina* and *The Servant of Two Masters*. *La buona figliuola* (1756) was the most-performed opera of all his works, which were set to music many times. In this opera, the virtuous Cecchina loves a man of rank whom she can only marry when she herself is of noble blood, as she also turns out to be.

exportable because of their use of local dialect.

The *opera buffa* owed its success largely to the already established popularity of the *commedia dell'arte*, which had long been socially acceptable and was performed in theaters. In Paris, for example, the *Comédie Italienne* had played since 1680 in their own house, the Théâtre Italien, with some interruptions. Crucial for the spread of *buffa* were itinerant opera ensembles and impresarios, such as Giovanni Battista Locatelli, who made guest appearances with his troupe in such cities as Prague and St. Petersburg, or the Venetians Angelo and Pietro Mingotti, who traveled as far as Hamburg and Copenhagen.

In the realm of theater, it was thanks to Carlo Goldoni that the half-masks were removed from the figures in the *commedia dell'arte*, giving them greater reality ("life under the mask is like fire under ashes"). Out from behind the masks appeared characters, that, while still quite stereotypical, were predestined to be instrumental in resuscitating such characters as the moody servant from the older Italian operas. Even if hardly any *buffo* operas actually adopted specific individual *commedia dell'arte* figures, such as the Venetian Pantalone, the commedia dell'arte provided the prototype, which endured even into the 19th century in such figures as "Don Pasquale."

Among the stock characters of the *opera buffa* belong the young lovers, usually a noble pair, as though lifted out of the *opera seria* and portrayed musically with the means of the *opera seria*, often for satirical purposes. Members of the lower classes, whose roles range from the crudely comical to the endearingly flirtatious but never extend to the heroic, round out the play. Cunning maids and servants, the secret heroes since time immemorial, advance to the status of true protagonists. A good deal of the entertainment value of these productions stemmed from the tension between such *parti buffe* and *parti serie*, heightened by the richly varied duets and ensembles which become the proper domain of the *opera buffa*. The intermediate finale and the finale form the climaxes, breaking up the schematic succession of songs by their dramatic musical intensity. The conclusions of acts were skillfully interwoven, complex ensemble scenes in which the threads of the plot thickened, keeping

Characters from the commedia dell'arte as Meissen porcelain figures.

pace with the increasing tempo and density of the music. Such act conclusions were composed by Baldassare Galuppi (the so-called chain finale) and Niccolò Piccini (the multisectional, or *rondo*, finale).

Just as the through-composed finale was characteristic of the *opera buffa*, so was the use of realistic voice ranges. It was only the character of the lover, as long as he was of the nobility, that was written in the alto or soprano range in the style of the *primo uomo* of the *opera seria*. As for the rest of the male roles, the use of the tenor and increasingly the bass became to be expected.

Georg Friedrich Handel lived in London after 1712, where he composed 35 Italian operas in almost 30 years.

Georg Friedrich Handel, a harpsichordist and violinist, left his native home of Halle (Saale) at the age of nineteen for Hamburg and the *Gänsemarktoper*. Here, after a short time, his own first opera (*Almira*, 1705) was performed. Modeled on the predilections of his age, this work contained 15 Italian arias, adapted by Friedrich Christian Feustking more or less unchanged from the Venetian libretto of Giulio Pancieri.

Handel next spent several years in Italy, where he met with Scarlatti and Steffani and composed two operas: *Rodrigo* (1707, in Florence) and *Agrippina*

(1709, in Venice). On Steffani's recommendation, Handel went to Hannover in 1710 as music director and in the same year took his first trip to England. On February 24, 1711, his opera *Rinaldo* was performed at the Queen's Theater on the Haymarket in London; it was a spectacular success. Handel decided to make London his permanent residence in 1712; there, in less than thirty years, he wrote another thirty-five operas. As the resident composer of an opera company in which he was also to become a partner, Handel engaged prima donnas such as Margherita Durastanti (*Radamisto*, 1720), Francesca Cuzzoni (*Rodelinda*, 1725), and Faustina Bordoni, who would later marry German composer Johann Adolf Hasse. Bordoni and Cuzzoni were known to be bitter rivals who engaged in real singing duels on stage that degenerated into violent scuffles at the instigation of the howling audience (which would later be parodied in John Gay's *Beggar's Opera*). Handel managed to engage a real "superstar," the alto castrato Francesco Bernardi, called Senesino, for *Giulio Cesare* (1724) and *Orlando* (1733), but he lost him in 1733 when Bernardi joined the rival opera company under Nicola Porpora, the "Opera of the Nobility," where the great Farinelli also sang. Both companies went bankrupt in 1737. Handel's efforts to make a new beginning failed: Both of his last operas *Imeneo* (1740) and *Deidamia* (1741) were unsuccessful, and Handel only managed to attain the level of his earlier triumphs in his oratorios: *Messiah* (1742) and *Judas Maccabaeus* (1747).

In their music and structure, Handel's operas are essentially Italian, but there are also traces of French influence. The overtures, for example, have more in common with Lully than with Scarlatti, and in a work such as *Ariodante* (premiered in 1735) the many duets, choruses, and ballets are "French," whereas the moresca at the end of the second act is clearly in the tradition of the English masque. German elements are also evident in, for example, some melodic borrowings from Reinhard Keiser. Handel also never entirely lost his counterpoint abilities, having been trained in German choirmaster tradition. This was, of course, all to the best, for the orchestral parts are much more detailed than in the works of Italian contemporaries.

In terms of his texts, Handel's operas represent a cross-section of the Italian librettos of the 17th and early 18th centuries. Three are based on Metastasio's dramatic poetry: *Siroe* (1728), *Poro* (1731), and *Ezio* (1732). One is taken from a libretto by Zeno, *Faramondo* (1737). Handel's

In 1959, Handel's *Alcina* was recorded by the Westdeutscher Rundfunk, who used authentic Baroque instruments. This was a milestone in the history of so-called historical performances, not unlike the production of Monteverdi's *L'Orfeo* under August Wenzinger four years earlier at the tenth *Sommerliche Musiktage* (Summer music festival) in Hitzacker, West Germany.

Georg Friedrich Händel

Zum Gedächtnis seines Todestages vor 200 Jahren veranstaltete der Westdeutsche Rundfunk am 15. Mai 1959 eine konzertante Aufführung der

Alcina

Oper in drei Akten

Die Cappella Coloniensis — Leitung Ferdinand Leitner

Deutsche Zwischentexte von Günter Haußwald und Eigel Kruttge

Alcina	Joan Sutherland, Sopran
Ruggiero	Fritz Wunderlich, Tenor
Morgana, Alcinas Schwester	Jeannette van Dijck, Sopran
Bradamante, Braut des Ruggiero	Norma Procter, Alt
Oronte, Feldherr der Alcina	Nicola Monti, Tenor
Melisso, Gefolgsmann Bradamantes	Thomas Hemsley, Baß
Sprecher	Paul Hoffmann

Der Kölner Rundfunkchor — Chordirektor Bernhard Zimmermann

A Baroque version of *Ariodante*, performed at the Göttingen Handel Festival in 1995 (the ballet finale of the second act with the New York Baroque Dance Company). In Göttingen, under the direction of the art historian Oskar Hagen, a staged production of a Handel opera was performed in June 1920, the first such performance since 1755. Göttingen has remained a center for the renaissance of Handel's operas in the 20th century.

favorite poet, however, was Nicolo Francesco Haym. While not a master of his trade, he did have the advantage of residing in London. For many of Handel's operas the authors of the texts, or rather the adapters of Italian source material, remain unknown. For *Tolomeo* (1728), it is known that Haym adapted, and drastically shortened, material already used by Domenico Scarlatti.

Tolomeo was produced in an attempt to save Handel's first London opera company, the Royal Academy, which at that time was facing bankruptcy. Senesino sang the title role, and the two rivaling prima donnas Cuzzoni and Bordoni were engaged to win back the audience. The public, however, was apparently more taken by the parody produced on the London stage: *The Beggar's Opera*. This ballad opera, a pastiche of Italian operas with satirical texts by John Gay and music by Johann Christoph Pepusch (including many Scottish folk songs and a march from *Rinaldo*) became the greatest success in the history of English theater, whereas *Tolomeo* sealed the demise of the Royal Academy.

In the following year, however, Handel tried to reawaken the interest of the London public for the *opera seria*, and for a while he was successful. But the satirists were never far behind. Parodies like *The Dragon of Wantley* by John Frederick Lampes (the prototype was *Giustino*), performed in 1737, were triumphant. Perhaps they were why Handel tried to distance himself from the *opera seria* in his own final operas.

The beginning of the Xerxes aria, "Ombra mai fu," at the premiere on April 15, 1738, sung by the castrato Gaetano Caffarelli (from the printed edition that appeared in London in the same year).

Fritz Wunderlich sang the part of Ruggiero (transposed for tenor) in a 1959 production of the Westdeutscher Rundfunk. This role was originally written for soprano and was sung by the famous castrato Giovanni Carestini at its premiere in 1735.

In 1738 he composed *Serse* (Xerxes), with a text based on an older Venetian libretto by Niccolò Minato. Here the servant Elviro provides an ironic break from the conventions of the genre, as does the opening scene in which Xerxes rests in the shadow of a plane tree. The shadow, conventionally a symbol of death or an occasion for necromancy (*umbra scene*), signifies here nothing more than a pleasing, actually a thoroughly mundane moment, awakening a desire for an amorous adventure in the weak heart of the royal hero. Hardly any piece of music has been so misunderstood by posterity as this aria in larghetto tempo, which came to be known as "Handel's Largo," causing outbreaks of sentimental and pseudo-religious fervor.

Jean-Philippe Rameau, a music theorist and a composer, was a central figure in the musical world of his time.

Rameau and the *querelle des bouffons*

In France, Jean-Philippe Rameau, who only became interested in opera in his mid-forties, took up the *tragédie lyrique* created by Lully and refined it in a very unique way, leaving the basic framework of the genre untouched. His opera *Hippolyte et Aricie* (with text by Abbé Pelegrin, 1733) immediately provoked protest from traditionalists, who felt that the smooth flow of the classical prototype was impaired through the overly emotional, aria-like declamatory passages and through the predominance of purely instrumental movements. And the critics were not entirely wrong, for Rameau did expand the orchestra's range of expression by his inclusion of wind instru-

The scenery, the stage mechanics, the lighting, and the costumes ... all surpassed in their tastefulness, splendor, and magnificence even the most beautiful things that had been seen here since the inauguration of the building. In the fifth act, the stage sets constituted a marvelous temple; its fluted columns were adorned with carbuncles and rubies, which shone like the brightest, flaming fire. The columns were placed on pedestals and had capitals; both made of the same precious metal. The vaulted ceiling that they supported was painted green and was decorated with fields of gold and silver and mosaics. ... A cupola of seemingly infinite height and dimensions formed the shrine, separated from the rest of the building through a balustrade. At the center of the shrine, a holy fire could be seen flickering on a beautiful altar. Finally, on both sides of the temple, there were wonderful galleries decorated with laurel wreaths, myrtle, and flowers. Here in this gorgeous temple the coronation and the marriage of Zoroastre took place.

Abbé Joseph de Laporte on the premiere of Zoroastre
at the Académie de Musique in Paris on December 5, 1749
(from Anecdotes dramatiques, *1775)*

ments. Rameau was a master of instrumentation and of emotional tone painting, consistently interpreting the action from the point of view of the musician-dramatist.

In *Zoroastre* (1749, text by Louis de Cahusac), the fourth of five surviving *tragédies lyriques*, Rameau abandoned the prologue, thereby enhancing the prominence of the overture, which evolved into a programmatic introduction to the dramatic events of the opera. Rameau noted in the libretto that the first part of this overture contains a strong, pathetic description of barbaric acts of violence and of the lamentation of the peoples in the kingdom of Zoroaster's adversary Abramane.

Despite Rameau's progressive musical language, by the middle of the century many considered the *tragédie lyrique*, the showpiece of French court culture, outdated. Rameau, then, suddenly found himself being defended by his former opponents: They lifted him on their standard, as it were, as the conserver of tradition in their resistance against the encroachment of the Italian *opera buffa*.

The alto Pierre Jelyotte sang the part of the magician in *Zoroastre* in Rameau's opera of the same name. Jelyotte, with the soprano Marie Fel, belonged among the celebrated stars of the Académie Royale de Musique, as the Paris opera was called since the days of Lully.

The occasion of this argument, which threatened to split the musical nation, was the 1746 Paris premiere of Pergolesi's *intermezzo La serva padrona*. The same piece was performed again in Paris in 1752 by Italian artists (called

Sketch of a costume, adorned with feathers by Jean Berain (Paris, 1673). The narrow waist is typical of Baroque fashion, but the short skirt of the "Indian," leaving bare knees, is unusual. Rameau's ballet opera, *Les Indes galantes*, from the year 1735, depicts the indigenous peoples of foreign places as "noble savages," an expression of the love of exotic milieus so typical of the period.

Festival performance of the opera *L'Arsace*, by Francesco Feo for the reopening of the Teatro Regio in Turin (1740), scenery by Giuseppe Galli-Bibiena. The orchestra consisted of about 30 musicians: 18 string players with one recorder or oboe, as well as two continuo groups with stringed basses, bassoon, and one harpsichord each. Two horns may be seen on the left. In the middle aisle and on the right in the pit, one can see servants bringing refreshments. Some members of the audience are looking at their librettos, one (left, bottom) is looking through an opera telescope at the stage.

bouffons), and was received with great enthusiasm; even Jean-Jacques Rousseau modeled his own *Le devin du village* on Pergolesi's successful work. This *intermède* became the prototype for the ingenuous, "natural" opera that accorded well with the ideals of the Enlightenment.

In the midst of Enlightenment debate, the "querelle des bouffons" even assumed a political dimension, engaging some of the leading intellectuals of the period. In 1754, the Italian opera troupe had to leave Paris, by order of the authorities. This overreaction only highlighted the fact that the *ancien régime* was beginning to topple, and with it the traditional cultural forms in which its image had been conveyed. Nevertheless, the operas of Rameau and even those of Lully would maintain their standing in Paris and Versailles through the 1770s.

Vaudeville and *opéra comique*

Rameau's mythological farce *Platée* (1745) represented an early attempt to create a comic counterpart to the *tragédie lyrique*. Unlike the conventional *comédie ballet*, the *comédie lyrique* uses the recitative in place of spoken dialogue. Nevertheless, in the development of the *opéra comique*, neither form played an important role; both were firmly anchored in the court tradition. Far more important was the influence of the Italian buffa and of the popular comedies performed in fairground booths (*Théâtres de la Foire*), lightened by vaudevilles and aria parodies. The decisive impulse for its further development was given by Rousseau and his "village prophet" (see *Le devin du village* above). Following the Italian conventions, Rousseau inserted recitatives into his one-act drama, even though he considered the French language ill-suited to them. As if to prove him right, the retention of spoken dialogue in lieu of recitative came to characterize the revised *opéra comique*, which soon won adherents abroad.

"Back to nature," Rousseau's motto, found expression in realistic scenarios and supposedly true-to-life characters enacted

The differences between the world of the court and world of the bourgeoisie are the subject of many comic operas. Such works as Favart's *Ninette à la cour* mark the beginning of a trend toward socially realistic costumes on the opera stage.

within themes from bourgeois dramas that were also common to *opera buffa*. One example is Goldoni's poetic drama, set by Piccinni, *La buona figliuola* (1760), based on Samuel Richardson's novel *Pamela or Virtue Rewarded*. Musically seen, *ariettes* and simple, song-like *nouveaux airs* replaced the grander arias ("nouveaux" in contrast to the well-known vaudevilles that were reworded according to need). The *opéras comiques*, the powerful competitors of the *Académie de Musique* performing in the *Palais Royal*, were housed in the old *Hôtel de Bourgogne*. Here, in 1762 the *Théâtre de la Foire* merged with the *Théâtre Italien*; in 1783 they moved into the newly built *Comédie Italienne* and soon changed its name to the *Opéra-Comique*, though also known as the *Salle Favart*.

Charles-Simon Favart, longstanding theater director, was the most successful librettist of the *Opéra-Comique* in the second half of the 18th century. Among the most important composers were the Italian Egidio Romualdo Duni, as well as François-André Danican Philidor, Pierre-Alexandre Monsigny, and André-Ernest-Modeste Grétry, born in Liège. Grétry first wrote light stories, set in a country milieu, then broadened his range to include more sentimental, bourgeois pieces (*comédie larmoyante*). His most successful works included the one-act *Lucile* (1769, text by Jean-François Marmontel, also based on Richardson's *Pamela*) and *Richard Coeur de Lion* (1784, text by Jean-Michel Sedaine), a historical subject foreshadowing the direction soon to be taken by the "rescue" or "shock-opera," a noncomical facet of the *opéra comique* at the time of the French Revolution.

Gluck and the opera reformation

Christoph Willibald Gluck, born in Germany to a family of Bohemian foresters, became the reformer of the serious opera, which had lost ground even outside France. His operas broke away from the artificiality of both the opera seria and the *tragédie lyrique*; instead, he led both to a new synthesis that was captivating because of its sublime simplicity. The poet Ranieri de' Calzabigi, once a follower of Metastasio who eventually became the latter's resolute opponent, was the driving force behind the new movement. In *Orfeo ed Euridice* (1762) and *Alceste* (1767), he provided Gluck with texts for two operas that were spectacularly successful in Vienna, and their renown even spread as far as Paris. Calzabigi's recipe for success featured a continuously straightforward line of action

Christoph Willibald Gluck and his dramatist Calzabigi treat music as an element more firmly at the service of drama in their opera reform.

My intention was to lead music back to its true purpose: it should support the changing scenes and emotions of the drama, without interrupting the action of the plot and distracting from its intensity through useless and superfluous ornamentation. I was also of the opinion that music should produce the same kind of effect as a careful, harmoniously arranged drawing: The vitality of colors, the happy distribution of light and shadows bring the figures to life, without disfiguring their contours. Therefore, I did not want to interrupt a character at the climax of a dialogue, forcing him to wait out the duration of a tedious *ritornello*, or to hold him fast in the middle of a word on a nice vowel, so that the virtuosity of his lovely voice in a lengthy *coloratura* could be admired, or to interrupt him through an orchestral piece to give him a breathing space for his cadenza.

Christoph Willibald Gluck on his opera reform
(from his Preface to the 1769 printed full score of Alceste)

without complicated intrigues, and a drastically curbed number of protagonists. Where Metastasio's dramas generally included six main characters, here were only three: Orfeo, Euridice, and Amor. Gluck replaced the inflexible structure of *recitativo secco* and *Da capo* aria with scenes that could develop flexibly and dynamically by intertwining *accompagnati*, song-like arias, almost without embellishment and emotional choruses.

The radio production of 1964 was an attempt to reconstruct the original tonal coloring of an 18th-century opera. This entailed using historical instruments. Not at all historically accurate was a baritone for the title role. Gluck originally wrote the part for a castrato, and in the Paris version for a tenor.

After an unsuccessful business venture as a partner in the Viennese Burgtheater, and after the relatively disappointing reception of his opera *Paride ed Elena* (1770, text by Calzabigi), Gluck decided to accept a position in France. He was chosen for the position to refute Rousseau's prejudices against French as a language for opera.

With the help of the poetically talented attaché of the French embassy in Vienna, the Marquis du Roullet, who in turn used a drama by Jean Racine, Gluck composed the *tragédie-opéra, Iphigénie en Aulide*, in 1774. The premiere catapulted Gluck in French opinion onto a pedestal with Lully and Rameau. Gluck's *Iphigénie* overture is reminiscent of Rameau: The mood of the piece presages the plot that is to follow, and, as in *Alceste*, the music fuses seamlessly with the first scene.

Anna Caterina Antonacci as "Armide" in a production of the Milan Scala for the opening of the 1996-97 season (production, decor, and costumes by Pier Luigi Pizzi; musical director Riccardo Muti).

Gluck repeated his earlier successes in Paris by producing French versions of his first two Viennese "reform-operas." He composed new recitatives, added ballet music (which he adopted in part from earlier operas), and rewrote the castrato part of Orfeo, giving it to a tenor. Gluck then went on to write three new works: *Armide* (1777, libretto by Quinault, a text that Lully had already set to music), *Iphigénie en Tauride* (1779, text by Nicolas-François Guillard), and the only moderately successful *drame lyrique*, *Echo et Narcisse* (1779, text by Ludwig Theodor von Tschudi).

Iphigénie en Tauride inadvertently made adversaries of Gluck, Piccinni, and François-

Joseph Gossec in a competition steered by external interests, a feud from which Gluck emerged victorious. Despite the many borrowings from earlier works, Gluck's *Iphigénie* was generally acclaimed a masterpiece. Tommaso Traëtta's composition and Piccinni's as well could not compare with Gluck's work, which may still be seen as one of the most successful reincarnations of the Euripides play, along with Goethe's theater piece of the same title.

Gluck, who had been musical director of the Mingotti opera troupe for several years, was strongly influenced by the Neapolitan school, as were most of the opera composers of his time. It was finally contact with the *opéra comique* that allowed him to veer off the well-trodden paths and to overcome the national differences that he himself had described as ridiculous. Gluck declared his commitment to an international music ("propre à toutes les nations") and to the pathos of true, simple, and noble passions, to the same concern for humanity that Ludwig van Beethoven was later to formulate in his works under the influence of the French Revolution.

Although younger by a half a century, Wolfgang Amadeus Mozart, like Gluck before him, was a child of the Italian opera scene. In

A program from La Scala in Milan for a production of *Armide*, an opera that united the tradition of tragédie lyrique with opera seria. In his overture, Gluck drew on an earlier work (*Telemaco*, 1765).

all his works, even when they are at their most original and unconventional, this influence remains evident. Mozart's genius can perhaps be seen most clearly in the fact that he brought about a fundamental renewal of the Italian opera without ever breaking with its traditions.

In his opera *Die Zauberflöte* (The Magic Flute), Mozart launched an independent German opera tradition, but this achievement

In the 19th century, when the castrati were a thing of the past, Gluck's *Orfeo* became a role for female singers in men's costumes. Anna Pauline Milder, a soprano, also sang the part of Leonore in the premiere of Beethoven's *Fidelio*. In 1805, she appeared as Tamino, which actually is a tenor range, in Mozart's *Magic Flute*.

seems almost insignificant next to that of *Don Giovanni*, for it is here that Mozart resurrected opera, which had degenerated into a *seria* and *buffa* stereotype. Mozart's *Don Giovanni* allowed opera to emerge as a complete genre and work of art. Mozart's late operas, in their complexity, transcend his own time. Their music seems to infiltrate all levels of expression and emotion, as though music and drama were dual illuminating forces that allow us to see inner and outer action and changes simultaneously. This is even true for *La clemenza di Tito*, which still bears the mark of Metastasio, offering a last peak of *opera seria* and even affording the castrato, already long past his glory, an honorable exit.

It is only since the 19th century that Wolfgang Amadeus Mozart has been characterized as the darling of the gods. During his own lifetime in Vienna, he was one of many successful composers, and his genius was often unrecognized by admirers and patrons alike: After the premiere of the *Entführung*, Emperor Joseph II remarked, "Ever so beautiful for our ears but too many notes, my dear Mozart!"

At the age of twelve, Mozart celebrated his debut as a composer of operas in Vienna with a German lyrical drama based on Rousseau's *Village Prophet*. The opera was called *Bastien und Bastienne* (1768, text based on Favart by Friedrich Wilhelm Weiskern and Andreas Schachtner); it was a harmless little work, performed privately, and no further interest was ever expressed in it. Mozart's next opera, *Mitridate, Re di Ponto*,

Picture-sheet with sketches from *Entführung aus dem Serail* (Berlin, circa 1829).

Mozart in Vienna

fared differently. A conventional *opera seria* complete with lengthy ballets, this work was composed for Italian clients. It debuted in a festive performance in Milan, lasted six hours, with Mozart himself directing from the first harpsichord, and was met with calls of bravo throughout the performance.

Joseph II was an enlightened monarch who initiated far-reaching reforms for his people and radically curbed the privileges of clergy and nobility. In 1787, he endowed Mozart with a yearly salary of 800 gulden so that "so rare a genius in the matter of music need not be forced to seek his remuneration and his livelihood abroad."

By the time he was 19, Mozart had composed nine theater works; five years, however, were to pass before he completed his next work, *Idomeneo, Re di Creta* (based on a text by Antoine Danchet adapted by librettist Giovanni Battista Varesco). *Idomeneo* was commissioned by the electoral prince of Bavaria, and was performed for the first time in Munich at the *Residenztheater* (Cuvilliés-Theater, 1781). Complete with ballet and choruses, in accordance with

Design of a set for *Idomeneo* (Wilhelm Kuhn, Cologne, 1878).

Design of a set for *Entführung* (Otto Reigbert, 20th century).

Costume sketches for *The Marriage of Figaro* from the Vienna Theater News (19th century).

Two great interpreters of Mozart in the roles of a lifetime: Lilli Lehmann as Donna Anna and Francisco d'Andrade as Don Giovanni. Lilli Lehmann began her career in 1870 as a *coloratura* in Berlin, then changed to dramatic music. She was known as the "primadonna assoluta," a sign of the high esteem accorded her. Similarly applauded was D'Andrade, who was oftened portrayed as Don Giovanni by artist Max Slevogt.

the wishes of the court, this *opera seria* became a decided success, and this success tempted Mozart to break with his employers in Salzburg, leading to his decision to go to Vienna. At the behest of Emperor Joseph II, who wanted to establish a German opera in Vienna, Mozart wrote *Die Entführung aus dem Serail* (The Escape from the Seraglio, 1782, text based on Christoph Friedrich Bretzner by Johann Gottlieb Stephanie the younger). This German-language *buffa* with a fashionable Turkish atmosphere had spoken dialogue and a "vaudeville" finale in the style of the *opéra comique*.

At the beginning of 1783, Mozart met the librettist Lorenzo da Ponte, poet in residence of the newly founded Italian theater in Vienna. Da Ponte suggested to Mozart an adaptation of the French comedy by Pierre Augustin Caron de Beaumarchais, *La folle journée ou Le marriage de Figaro*. Mozart started work immediately although he had no commission for the opera. In fact, Giovanni Paisiello had already composed a brilliant version of a similar subject matter that was well-known in Vienna: *Il barbiere di Siviglia.*

Mozart seemed to have some pieces by Paisiello in mind when composing arias such as Figaro's famous cavatina "Se vuol ballare" or Cherubino's "Voi, che sapete."

The original theater performances of Beaumarchais' biting comedy about the revolt of a servant couple against their noble lord were banned. An aristocracy conscious of its position and privileges in a Europe feeling the reverberations of the American Revolution and readying for the French

Left: Basilio, the music teacher in *The Marriage of Figaro*; sketch by Hans Strohbach for a Mozart project (1932).

Right: Luigi Goffredo Zuccoli as Leporello (Paris, 1828).

Baritone Francisco D'Andrade was considered the ideal Don Giovanni. Here, he is shown with his servant Leporello in the famous graveyard scene (etching by Max Slevogt, 1920).

Papageno's aria "Ein Mädchen oder Weibchen ...," in an etching by Max Slevogt (1920).

Sky filled with stars above the Queen of the Night; set design by Simon Quaglio (Munich, 1818).

Revolution was hardly likely to laugh at such subversive plots. Nonetheless, the emperor himself, despite some misgivings, allowed the performance of *Le nozze di Figaro* (The Marriage of Figaro), overriding criticism and the opposition of Mozart's rivals. At the premiere on May 1, 1786, the audience was divided, some rudely denouncing, others enthusiastically praising the work. In Prague, where the work was soon also produced, an unprecedented Figaro fervor erupted. Naturally, Mozart's next opera was then commissioned in Prague: *Don Giovanni* (text by da Ponte based on Giovanni Bertati) was just as successful as *Figaro* at its premiere on the October 29, 1787 in the National Theater in Prague.

At the special request of the emperor, *Don Giovanni* was performed in Vienna a short time later but met with somewhat less enthusiasm than it had inspired in Prague. It was performed only fifteen times in 1788 and not at all for many years after that. *Le nozze di Figaro* was performed twenty times between 1786 and 1790, while Antonio Salieri's popular opera *Axur, Re d'Ormus* and Paisiello's *Barbiere*

The Magic Flute in a modern setting: scenery by Max Bignens (top, Munich, 1971) and Roland Topor (bottom, Essen, 1990).

In 1801 the Theater an der Wien opened; it could seat more than 2,000 people. It replaced Emanuel Schikaneder's Freihaustheater auf der Wieden.

were performed a total of forty-two and sixty times, respectively, between 1783 and 1790.

In 1789 the emperor again commissioned Mozart to compose an opera. *Così fan tutte*, with libretto by da Ponte, had its promising premiere on January 26, 1790 in the *Burgtheater* on the evening before Mozart's thirty-fourth birthday. Unfortunately, Joseph II died barely a month later, and with the nation officially in a period of mourning, *Così* could no longer be performed. Even after the period of mourning had passed, the opera was only performed five more times during Mozart's lifetime.

While still working on *Die Zauberflöte* (*The Magic Flute*), which would be Mozart's last opera, with text by actor/theater manager Emanuel Schikaneder, Mozart received a new commission from Prague for a festive opera for September 6, 1791, the day on which the new Emperor Leopold II was to be crowned King of Bohemia. In only seven weeks Mozart finished *La clemenza di Tito*, a classical *opera seria* based on Metastasio (the text was adapted by Caterino Mazzolà). On September 31, 1791, five weeks before his death at the age of thirty-six, *The Magic Flute* premiered at Schikaneder's

theater on the outskirts of Vienna in the *Freihaustheater auf der Wieden.*

Unlike the three Da Ponte operas, which as perfect music dramas represent the culmination of the Italian opera tradition, *The Magic Flute* seems like an immature prototype for a German lyric drama with *seria* inserts. It remains something of a cross between a "mechanical comedy," magic story or fairy tale, and a critical contemporary revue. Mozart's music alone ensures that, despite all the contradictions inherent in the work, a certain charm and harmonious quality remain. The overture clearly portrays the tension between the realm of the Queen of the Night and the world of Sarastro's Masons, though it is an ambiguous tension at best. Despite dramatic weaknesses, *The Magic Flute* remains the most successful of Mozart's operas.

Elisa Müller as Sextus (Breslau, 1805) in Mozart's *Tito*. Sextus is a classical castrato role, as is the role of his friend Annius, which, however, was sung by a soprano, even at the premiere.

Sketch by Giorgio Fuentes of a stage scene for *Tito* (Frankfurt, 19th century).

Ludwig van Beethoven and Wilhelmine Schröder-Devrient at a rehearsal for *Fidelio.* Whether rehearsals of this type were actually ever held is more than doubtful. But soon after her debut as Pamina in Mozart's *Magic Flute* (Vienna, 1821), the soprano became the most popular Leonore of her time.

Opera and politics:
The seeds of nationalistic operas

On the 13th of October, 1806, as Napoleon Bonaparte passed through the city of Jena en route to his victory over the Prussians, philosopher Georg Wilhelm Friedrich Hegel felt he was watching the "spirit of the age" ride by: "What an individual ... concentrated here into one point and sitting on a horse, but spreading out over the entire world and dominating it." Through the triumphs of Napoleon, the values of the French Revolution seemed to take hold throughout Europe—ideas to which even Ludwig van Beethoven felt drawn, although his enthusiasm for Napoleon ended abruptly when Napoleon crowned himself emperor. The self-assertive spirit of Beethoven's Third Symphony, which the composer originally intended to dedicate to Napoleon, nevertheless testified to the "élan terrible" of French revolutionary music.

The theme dominating the first movement of the Third Symphony (subtitled "Eroica"), a kind of signaling motif, had already been heard in the introduction to Mozart's *Bastien und Bastienne.* This seems a peculiar coincidence, but since this singspiel was based on a text by Jean-Jacques Rousseau, it is natural also to wonder if the common musical substance also denotes common ideals. French military signals can also be heard in the "Leonore" overtures to Beethoven's only opera, *Fidelio.*

The story of *Fidelio* is based on an actual event witnessed personally by the author Jean Nicolas Bouilly: During the tumult of the French Revolution, a courageous woman, disguised as a man, managed to free her husband from prison. Bouilly's original libretto was first set to music by Pierre Gaveaux in 1798, and this version as well as the *Leonora ossia L'amore conjugale*, by Ferdinando Paër (which premiered in 1804), historicized the plot, removing the scene of action to the Spain of about 1500. Beethoven's librettists and adapters (Joseph Ferdinand von Sonnleithner, Stephan von Breuning, and Georg Friedrich Treitschke) kept Spain as the locale but brought the action back to the near contemporary. The premiere of *Fidelio oder die eheliche Liebe* on November 20, 1805 in Vienna's *Theater an der Wien* was a flop, in part because Beethoven himself conducted badly in the midst of his deteriorating hearing, and because the audience consisted mainly of officers of the French occupation army, who did not understand the language. Four months later a new version

Wilhelmine Schröder-Devrient as Fidelio/Leonore opposing Don Pizarro, the sinister director of the state prison, in order to protect her beloved Florestan ("First, kill his wife!").

The Spanish state prison: stage set by Lorenzo Sacchetti for the premiere of Beethoven's *Fidelio* at the Theater an der Wien (1805).

called *Leonore* (Beethoven's preferred title, which he had earlier relinquished in favor of *Fidelio*, to avoid confusion with earlier settings of the Bouilly text) was performed; this version consisted of two instead of three acts and was better received. But the first real breakthrough for the piece came with its third version in 1814.

As a classic "rescue opera," *Fidelio* falls in the tradition of the most popular type of *opéra comique* of the revolutionary age, but the strong bourgeois morality informing its vision of freedom cannot be overlooked. In fact, one can hardly imagine a greater contrast than that between this "panegyric on married love" and Mozart's pre-Revolution operas with librettist da Ponte, the ultimate expression of a supposedly immoral age.

Singspiel and operas in the German-speaking world

In Vienna from the 1760s onward, works of *opera buffa* and *opéra comique* inspired German-language imitations. One of the most successful of these was the *singspiel* (literally the "singing

A Baroque backstage comedy returns with a vengeance: *L'Opera seria* by Florian Leopold Gassmann (Vienna, 1769, text by Ranieri de' Calzabigi). After its "excavation" by René Jacobs, an early-music specialist, this genre parody was revived in a 1994 coproduction of the Berlin State Opera and the Schwetzingen Festival, staging by Jean-Louis Martinoty. The picture shows Richard Croft, Janet Williams, and Curtis Rayam at the Innsbruck Festival.

play," also called light opera)
Der Rauchfangkehrer,
an opera composed by
Antonio Salieri at the request
of the emperor in 1781 (with
a libretto by Leopold von
Auenbrugger). Still more
renowned was *Doktor und
Apotheker* by Karl Ditters von
Dittersdorf (1786, libretto by Johann Gottlieb
Stephanie, the younger). It completely surpassed in acclaim Mozart's *Figaro,* which had
premiered just shortly before, and within a few
years was performed many times in different
countries and different languages, becoming the
first German opera to achieve international
success.

Marie-Thérèse Maillard
in the *tragédie lyrique
Tarare* (1787, text by
Beaumarchais), Antonio
Salieri's second
successful opera in
Paris. His first success,
Les Danaides (1784),
was achieved with the
help of Gluck, who was
billed as coauthor even
though Salieri wrote it
alone. When he
presented *Axur, Re
d'Ormus* (the Italian
version of *Tarare*) in
Vienna in 1788, Salieri
appeared to such
advantage that he was
appointed that same
year court composer
and conductor. Once
the pupil of Florian
Gassmann, Salieri
became one of the
most sought-after
composition teachers in
Vienna. Both Beethoven
and Liszt were among
his pupils.

   Only a handful of German works can really
compete on the level of the *opera seria. Günther
von Schwarzburg* by Ignaz Holzbauer (performed
in Mannheim in 1777, to a libretto by Anton
Klein) perhaps comes closest, but in musical
terms it remains totally indebted to its Italian
models, as does Anton Schweitzer's *Alceste*
(produced in Weimar in 1773, with text by
Christoph Martin Wieland). The *accompagnati* in
Holzbauer's opera are noteworthy in that they
often are integrated with the *recitativo secco* and
aria, suggesting their through-composed form.
Even the extremely weak libretto later took on
significance in relation to upcoming events
because it treated a German and extremely
patriotic subject. Mozart, who became familiar
with this work in a production by the excellent
Mannheim orchestra, reported to his father:
"Holzbauer's music is very beautiful. The poetry

Johann Adam Hiller was one of the leaders in Leipzig musical circles. He was a singing teacher, founder of the Gewandhaus concerts, and, as the Thomascantor, the third successor of Johann Sebastian Bach. He also composed *Lottchen am Hofe* (Leipzig, 1767, text by Christian Felix Weisse based on Favart's *Ninette à la cour*), a singspiel devoid of any sophisticated arias, but nonetheless typical of early German operetta and pioneering in its own way. Although operettas grew out of popular comedies with added songs and tended toward simple strophic melodies, arias and ensembles (vaudeville finales) in the style of opera buffa and opéra comique were also widely used.

is not worthy of such music. But most of all, I wonder how an old man like Holzbauer can still have so much spirit; the fire in his music is incredible."

Rousseau's *scène lyrique Pygmalion* (performed in Lyon, France, in 1770) represented an attempt to steer a middle course between drama and opera; Georg Anton Benda, the *kapellmeister* of the Prussian court at Gotha, similarly strove in his works to achieve this ideal. Where Rousseau used music to interpret emotions, though not as background to text recitations and pantomimes, in Benda's works instrumental and spoken parts could overlap. In his *Ariadne auf Naxos* (with a libretto by Johann Christian Brandes, performed in Gotha in 1775), *Medea* (libretto by Friedrich Wilhelm Gotter, performed in Leipzig in 1775), and in similar works of other poets and composers up to the turn of the century—even the German literary giant Goethe experimented for a time with the new form of the melodrama—Germany experienced a brief flowering of this genre. Still, these few works cannot change the fact that, until the beginning of the Romantic Age, the development of an independent German opera never progressed beyond some promising baby steps. In the long run, only Mozart's *Magic Flute* and Beethoven's

Ariadne auf Naxos. Engraving from the *Gotha Theater Calendar* for the year 1766.

> Only in true romanticism does the comic mix with the tragic so harmoniously that both melt into a single total effect, gripping the mind and heart of the listener in a special and wonderful way.
>
> *E.Th.A. Hoffmann*, The Poet and the Composer, *1813*

Fidelio would maintain their standing. They laid the foundation for the romantic German opera in all its variety from the musical fairy tale to the ideological drama.

It was Ernst Theodor Amadeus Hoffmann, known as "Gespenster-Hoffmann," "Ghost-Hoffmann," who began the tradition. Not only was he one of the leading proponents of Romantic literature, but also, as a critic, conductor, and composer, he played a formative role in the musical life of his times.

German operas in Berlin and Dresden

Hoffmann's most important plays are based on texts by other authors: *Undine* is from a novel by Friedrich de la Motte Fouqué, one of the most popular German writers of the early 19th century, who was equally admired outside his native country. The basic ingredients of his works were Nordic myths, fairy tales, medieval knights, and a large dose of fantasy; these combined in *Undine* to form a kind of concentrate, yielding a seemingly bottomless well of material for romantic operas. The sensational premiere took place on August 3, 1816 in the *Schauspielhaus am Gendarmenmarkt*, the second large theater in Berlin (the other one

Francesco Morlacchi composed about twenty conventional operas seria and buffa. As conductor of the Italian Court Opera in Dresden, he held a higher position than the conductor of the German Opera, Carl Maria von Weber.

Teresa Belloc-Giorgi as Donna Aurora in Morlacchi's opera of the same name (Milan, 1821, text by Felice Romani).

83

Carl Maria von Weber as conductor of his opera *Freischütz* in London. Weber had certain idiosyncrasies as an orchestra teacher and conductor: To make his directions more clear, he used a rolled up piece of music instead of a baton, which only slowly became standard equipment. In a letter of recommendation to the King of Prussia, Count Brühl, the theater director in Berlin, wrote of Weber: "As for conducting an orchestra, I dare assert that there are very few who could be considered his equal."

at the time was the *Königliches Opernhaus unter den Linden*).

Although Dresden had traditionally been the stronghold of Italian operas, it became the home of the German Romantic opera through the influence and works of Hoffmann, Carl Maria von Weber, and Richard Wagner. Weber was appointed musical director of Dresden's newly equipped *Deutsche Oper* in 1816; he brought to this post his valuable experience in Prague, where, as conductor of the *Ständetheater*, he had produced works such as Beethoven's *Fidelio* and Louis Spohr's *Faust* (1816, with text by Joseph Karl Bernard). Spohr's *Faust* remains basically a Viennese *singspiel*, even though one can hear unmistakeable echoes of Mozart, for example, in the dance music at the end of the second act, which is reminiscent of the famous festive finale of the first act of *Don Giovanni*. Weber's first operas as well fall within the framework of the *singspiel*. Even *Der Freischütz* (The Marksman), with text by Friedrich Kind based on a short story from August Apel and Friedrich Laun's *Gespensterbuch* (Book of Ghosts), remains in its basic structure a conventional *singspiel* with folksy melodies. Even so, it served as a kind of "big bang" in German musical theater thanks to Weber's exceptional sense for drama and artistic instrumentation, skills that disclose his genius as a conductor and his long experience in theatrical staging. One of his greatest achievements is the scene at the close of act II, the wolf's glen scene, in which the stirring depiction of nature and the melodramatic, haunted stage action culminate in the darkest of eerily romantic moments. The premiere in the newly reopened Berlin *Schauspielhaus* on June 18, 1821, was hailed by all as a triumph of German opera, while pieces such as the "Chorus of the Bridesmaids" became popular melodies overnight, making Weber one of the most popular composers of his day. Gasparo Spontini, formerly court conductor and composer to Napoleon, now music director in Berlin, found himself eclipsed.

Filled with ambition to confirm and surpass his great success, Weber composed his next opera, *Euryanthe*, in which he diverged from the structure

Max and Kaspar pouring the seven magic bullets. A contemporary illustration of the wolf's glen scene (Carl Lieber, 1824).

Gasparo Spontini, a co-inventor of grand opera, had been the first conductor of the Prussian court since 1820. In 1827, for the marriage of the prince in Berlin, a German-language classic example of this new genre was presented, *Agnes von Hohenstaufen*, with text by Ernst Raupach. Despite its clever instrumentation, monumental cast, and elaborate staging, the opera was only moderately successful.

of the *singspiel*, following the example of Spohr's *Jessonda* (performed in Kassel, 1823, with text by Eduard Heinrich Gehe), a lyrical rescue opera in Indian disguise. In *Jessonda*, a Portuguese officer saves the heroine from the widow's pyre at the last minute. Similarly, *Euryanthe* is a romantic knightly drama, filled with curiosities (a poisoned ring, a giant snake) that were partly authorized by Weber himself. Unfortunately, the shortcomings of the text (written by Helmina von Chézy together with the composer) detract from what was actually a successful attempt to create a through-composed opera to such an extent that, despite the successful premiere (in Vienna on October 25, 1823), *Euryanthe* became the foster child of opera repertoire. Only the overture is performed with any regularity, giving some insight into the great musical wealth of this work.

In Weber's last work, *Oberon,* the composer again took a step backward on the path toward grand opera. The truth is that the disjointed text left him little choice. Weber was seriously ill at the time but he had accepted a lucrative offer from London and composed about twenty pieces and a programmatic overture (the introductory horn

A set design by Karl Friedrich Schinkel, the great Berlin architect and stage designer, for Spontini's *Olympia* (Paris, 1816, with text by Michael Dieulafoy and Charles Brifaut based on Voltaire) in a new translation by E.Th.A. Hoffmann. This production marked the beginning of Spontini's career in Berlin (1821).

signal recurs thematically throughout the opera) for James Robinson Planché's sequence of scenes in the style of the older "semi-operas." Planché's work was based on themes from an epic poem by Christoph Martin Wieland, as well as from Shakespeare's *Midsummer Night's Dream*

A scene from *Euryanthe* with Wilhelmine Schröder-Devrient in the title role. Although Count Adolar seeks to take her life, Euryanthe protects him from a serpent (Dresden, 1824). Schröder-Devrient also sang Venus in the Dresden premiere of Wagner's *Tannhäuser*.

and *The Tempest*. Only a few weeks after he conducted the premiere (August 12, 1826), Weber died in London of tuberculosis at the age of thirty-nine. Despite the *singspiel* form and the prolonged spoken passages, Weber's *Oberon* remains a milestone in the development of the Romantic opera. In no previous work had the orchestra been so well differentiated and so important to the meaning as it is here. As proof, the spectrum of later composers who acknowledged their indebtedness to Weber included Hector Berlioz and Richard Wagner, Gustav Mahler and Claude Debussy, and even Igor Stravinsky, all of whom were accomplished masters of instrumentation.

Oberon's grove. Painting by Franz Angelo Rottonara (Wiesbaden, 1900, based on a stage set designed by Hans Kautsky).

Although Franz Schubert also contributed to the fund of German operas, his works were disregarded for a long time. Only three of over a dozen, in part unfinished, works were performed during his lifetime. They included *singspiels*, or "farces with songs," as well as melodramas and "heroic-romantic operas." Their neglect was due on the one hand to Schubert's inability to establish himself in the professional, Italian-biased opera world of Vienna. On the other hand, the librettos are dilettantish, the works of friends and hobby poets, such as Franz von Schober (*Alfonso und Estrella*, 1822, premiered in Weimar in 1854) and Joseph Kupelwieser (*Fierabras*, 1823, premiered in Karlsruhe in 1897). Only recently has a still-tentative Schubert renaissance begun.

One direct successor of Weber was Heinrich Marschner, who had a strong influence on Richard Wagner in his own right. Marschner's "dialogue operas" are a mixture of the *singspiel* (dialogue form) and the grand opera (scene blocks structured musically); they are characterized by musical depictions of nature and of supernatural apparitions. Marschner used vocal songs in the style of folk melodies, as well as *accompagnati* and arias, enlivened with melodramatic pieces. Works such as *Der Vampyr* (Leipzig, 1828, text by Wilhelm August Wohlbrück), *Der Templer und die Jüdin* (Leipzig, 1829, text by Wohlbrück based on Walter Scott's

Ivanhoe), and *Hans Heiling* (Berlin, 1833, text by Eduard Devrient) were very successful even beyond the German theaters of the composer's own time.

Aside from Marschner, among the composers of the generation

Albert Lortzing was an actor and singer ("second tenor and buffa parts") as well as a composer. He first encountered the material of *Zar und Zimmermann* (the story had already been set to music a number of times, including a version by Donizetti) as an actor in the role of Chateauneauf. When his own opera premiered in Leipzig, he sang the role of the young Russian deserter Peter Ivanov, who is mistaken for the tsar at a Dutch dock. Peter the Great's incognito visit to the Netherlands to study shipbuilding is historically verified.

between Weber and Wagner is Albert Lortzing, whose works are performed by today's opera companies more than are any of his contemporaries. Lortzing's *Zar und Zimmermann* (Leipzig 1837, text by Lortzing) and *Der Wildschütz oder Die Stimme der Natur* (Leipzig, 1842, text by the composer based on *Der Rehbock* by August von Kotzebue) were prime examples of the genre of the traditional German folk opera, which derived a good deal of its humor from the crassly exaggerated contrast between country and city folk, or between in their social stations. Two comic operas by Otto Nicolai and Friedrich von Flotow received even greater international acclaim than Lortzing's works. In *Die lustigen Weiber von Windsor* (Berlin, 1849, with text by Salomon Hermann Mosenthal based on Shakespeare's *Merry Wives of Windsor*), Nicolai, who had also been successful with Italian operas, managed to unite the virtues of Italian and German operas, according to his conviction: "One must have German schooling, that is the prime requisite; but one must add Italian lightness." Friedrich von Flotow's successful opera, *Martha oder Der Markt zu Richmond* (Martha, or The Marquise of Richmond) (Vienna, 1847, text by Friedrich Wilhelm Riese) is everything but ponderous, although it is not immune to touches of sentimentality and breaks with the customary spoken dialogues of the *singspiel* through its pleasantly conversational recitatives.

When Richard Wagner arrived upon the scene, he managed to overshadow almost all the other 19th century opera composers. Even in his own day, his works were so widely acclaimed that his popularity gave rise to a regular Wagner cult. To this day Wagner's musical and extramusical concerns have had an enormous influence on the opera world.

Richard Wagner.
Etching by Johann Leonhard Raab after an 1871 oil painting by Franz von Lenbach.

The strength of Richard Wagner's unique position among the composers of the 19th century is based not only on his musical but also on his literary career. Wagner was his own librettist and wrote many essays, polemical articles, short stories, and works on music theory. His first works for the stage, *Die Hochzeit* (The Marriage, a fragment) and *Die Feen* (The Fairies), were written while he was choir director in Würzburg (1833–1834). He continued his career as *kapellmeister* in places such as the central German city of Magdeburg (where he created *Das Liebesverbot* [The Ban on Love] in 1836, with a text based on Shakespeare's *Measure for Measure*) and the Latvian capital of Riga. His engagement in Riga

Ludwig II, King of Bavaria, as the "knight of the swan" (in Wagner's *Lohengrin*) in a contemporary newspaper caricature.

came to an abrupt end when the theater went bankrupt, and Wagner, deeply in debt himself, fled by ship to London and from there to Paris. There he wrote

St. Mark's Square in Venice. Sketch of a set design for *Catarina Cornaro* by Franz Lachner (Munich, 1841). As kapellmeister at the court theater and head music director (since 1856), Lachner had been at the peak of Munich's musical circles until the overwhelming ascension in 1864 of his rival Richard Wagner, who enjoyed the special favor of the king.

Wagner's Operas

Wagner expresses his gratitude to Ludwig II, who sent him word on May 3, 1864, that he would support him generously from then on:
"I send you these tears of heavenly emotion to tell you that now the wonders of poetry, like a divine reality, have entered my poor life, needy of love!—And this life, its final poems and tones, now belong to you, my gracious young king: treat them as if they were your own."

The Festival Theater in Bayreuth opened in 1876. One interesting and unusual feature of the theater is the invisible orchestra: a hood, of sorts, arches over the deep orchestra pit, allowing a dark tonal quality that is often described as mystic. An important element of the Bayreuth tonal nuances are the Wagner tubas, deep brass instruments blown with a bugle mouthpiece, specially constructed for the *Ring*.

Dresden, in which he participated as a personal friend and supporter of Mikhail Bakunin, Wagner was forced to leave Saxony. Now an outlaw in his homeland, Wagner spent the next few years mainly in Switzerland.

In 1864, his desolate financial situation reversed 180 degrees when King Ludwig II of Bavaria, a fervent admirer of Wagner's *Lohengrin*, decided to back Wagner and his opera schemes with enormous sums of money.

Rienzi and—still in the throes of his stormy voyage over the sea—*Der fliegende Holländer* (The Flying Dutchman). *Rienzi, der letzte der Tribunen* (Rienzi, the Last Tribune) was a great success when it premiered in 1842 in Dresden; one year later Wagner produced his, at first, less successful *Holländer* and took over the post of court conductor and composer. After the revolution of 1848–1849 and uprisings in

Giuseppe Siboni as the title character in Spontini's *Ferdinand Cortez* (Vienna, 1812).

Tannhäuser figurine by Josef Flüggen (Bayreuth, 1891).

Four years after the cornerstone had been laid, the *Festspielhaus* in the German city of Bayreuth was inaugurated in 1876 with *Der Ring des Nibelungen* (The Ring of the Nibelung, most commonly known as the *Ring* cycle). Acclaimed around the world, the event also incurred so large a financial deficit that the next festival could not be held again until 1882, one year before Wagner's death. On this latter occasion, *Parsifal* was performed for the first time. Since then about every two years until 1914, then irregularly, and since 1951 annually, the Bayreuth Festival has been a world-class musical and social event.

Wagner described his *Rienzi* as a "great tragic opera." In it, he was consciously imitating the work of Giacomo Meyerbeer, who had heightened the classicism of Gasparo Spontini to the point of pomposity and had used Spontini's 1809 opera *Fernand Cortez* as a direct model. Wagner's next three operas—*Der fliegende Holländer* (Dresden, 1843),

Grace Bumbry as Venus in Wieland Wagner's 1961 production of *Tannhäuser*, one hundred years after its scandalous premiere in Paris. The critics celebrated the debut of the "black Venus," and praised Maurice Béjart's choreography.

Tannhäuser (Dresden, 1845), and *Lohengrin* (Weimar, 1850)—are all explicitly "romantic." Thematically, they begin to approach what would be the central concern of his later works: redemption through love, renunciation, or death.

In *Tristan und Isolde*, which premiered in Munich in 1865, Wagner pushes to the limits of tonality. His bold harmonies seem to delineate the psychological states of his protagonists almost seismographically, while leitmotifs reveal the inner, underlying connections. The drama is removed into the music; there is hardly any stage action. *Tristan* had been canceled in Vienna after 77 rehearsals but then Ludwig II made it possible for the work to premiere at the Munich Court Opera. Three years later *Die Meistersinger von Nürnberg* (The Mastersingers of

Johanna Jachmann-Wagner as Ortrud in *Lohengrin* (Berlin, 1859).

Nuremberg) also premiered there. *Die Meistersinger* was a comedy, set in late medieval Nuremberg and infused with a solemn earnestness. Its themes, again, are love and renunciation. But always in the forefront is the conflict suffered by the creative

Ludwig Schnorr von Carolsfeld as Lohengrin. The heroic tenor also sang in the premiere of *Tristan und Isolde*, with his wife Malwina.

After her debut in Bayreuth in 1954, Birgit Nilsson became the most sought-after interpreter of Wagner in the world, in intensely dramatic roles. As Isolde, she often sang with the tenor Wolfgang Windgassen.

An illustration by Michael Echter after the premiere of *Die Meistersinger* at the Königliches Hof and Nationaltheater in Munich.

A production of *Die Meistersinger* during the Third Reich: The poster shows the total absorption of Wagner into the Nazi regime. Adolf Hitler was a close friend of Wagner's descendants, regularly attended the Bayreuth Festival, and prided himself on owning the original full score of *Rienzi* (now lost).

Woman attendant of Gutrune: figurine by Carl-Emil Doepler (*Die Walküre*, Bayreuth, 1876).

Set designer Max Brückner with his brother Gotthold operated a large workshop, with connections all around the world, that also equipped the Wagner productions in Bayreuth. Brückner's naturalistic scenes were used for decades, although they did not completely mesh with Wagner's ideas of an "invisible setting," the equivalent of the "invisible orchestra." Wagner envisioned settings that "participate only as the silent, potential background and surroundings of a characteristic situation."

man in a world determined to achieve conformity. This artist's drama was to become in effect the German national opera.

The key work of Wagner's career is the Ring cycle, which consists of *Das Rheingold* (The Rhinegold, Munich, 1869), an opera in four scenes planned to be performed the evening before the other parts of the cycle, which were three three-act works, conceived on a diffuse, extensive plan: *Die Walküre* (The Valkyrie, Munich, 1870), *Siegfried* (Munich, 1870), and *Götterdämmerung* (Twilight of the Gods, Bayreuth, 1876). The entire cycle, then,

lasts about 16 hours. In the theater built especially for performances of the *Ring*, the Wagnerian utopia of the complete work of art (*Gesamtkunstwerk*—a phrase more or less coined by Wagner to describe his own work) of the future could be partially realized: "it should include all the different kinds of art, in order to use up or destroy each as a single type, so that paradoxically they all attain their highest goal, namely, the necessary and immediate depiction of perfected human nature."

The *Ring* tetralogy was first heard in its complete version on

Autograph of Lauritz Melchior as Siegmund at the first Bayreuth Festival after the First World War (*Die Walküre*, 1924).

Lauritz Melchior, the Danish tenor whose portrait adorned even cigarette packages, became an international star, continuing his career in Hollywood, where he appeared in some musical films.

Hedwig Reicher-Kindermann as Brünnhilde (touring in the *Ring* in 1882). Head dress and helmet disclose the affinity to Wilhelminian style.

August 13–17, 1876, at the opening of the first Bayreuth Festival. This epic, ending with the death of Siegfried and the conflagration of the world in the *Götterdämmerung*, is a mixture of the Icelandic Edda, a Middle High German epic of a mythological evil family, the *Nibelungenlied*, the philosophy of Arthur Schopenhauer, and some anarchic thoughts. Nevertheless, it has continued to be the subject of endless interpretations, which, regardless of the direction they take, attest to the unbroken relevance of Wagner's music dramas.

Where the *Ring's* criticism of a society consumed by its hunger for power may been seen as a political work despite its mythologizing, in *Parsifal*—which he himself considered his key work—Wagner moves into the domain of religion. Nevertheless, the theme of redemption, here in the guise of the legends surrounding King Arthur and

Set design for *Götterdämmerung* (Wildermann, Cologne, 1912).

subsumed with Christian symbolism, seems less susceptible to theological interpretations than to sexual-psychological ones.

The musical legacy of *Parsifal* lies mainly in an austere chromaticism characterizing much of the central act that would wield a strong influence upon the works of later generations of composers.

Wagner would not allow performances of what he called his "Bühnenweihfestspiel" (A Stage Dedication Festival) outside of Bayreuth, although some unauthorized performances took place, as in New York in 1903 and in concert form in London in 1884. But after the thirty-year term of copyright expired, the *Ring* was performed all over the world. In Bayreuth the first production of *Parsifal* remained unaltered on the program for 50 years; after the Second World War, Wagner's grandson Wieland Wagner insisted on a new production that at the time seemed revolutionary and modern, a radical break from 19th-century historicism and staging values. An oval disc as stage and effective lighting were the most important staging techniques of the "New Bayreuth."

Martha Mödl, the first Kundry in *Parsifal*, in Bayreuth after the Second World War, also acclaimed as Brünnhilde. The mezzo soprano was a celebrated Clytemnestra (in Richard Strauss's *Elektra*). At the age of 80, she sang the countess in Tchaikovsky's *The Queen of Spades*.

Klingsor. Sketch by Ewald Dülberg, (*Parsifal*, Hamburg, 1914).

Opéra comique and *Grand opéra* in the 19th century

According to Aristotle's hierarchical classification of types of drama, comedy falls somewhere between tragedy and farce. The *opéra comique* of circa 1800 did not comply with this classical definition. Choice of subject matter and productions both encompassed the comical and the terrible; the opera stage became a laboratory for experiments with the sentimental and the pathetic, with universal and topical, with timeless and contemporary subjects. The fact that dialogue was spoken, not sung—a general characteristic of the *opéra comique*—brought the opera closer to "comedy," that is, to theatrical comedy as originally understood by Aristotle. Nevertheless, a certain nostalgia persisted for the complete works of art of the past and for the splendor of the *opera seria* and the *tragédie lyrique*, from which, not long after the turn of the century, the elaborate *grand opéra* of Spontini, Auber, and Meyerbeer evolved.

Luigi Cherubini, who would later become director of the world-famous Paris Conservatory, contributed largely to the progress of the *opéra comique* with his *Lodoïska* (premiered in 1791 with text by Claude-François Fillette-Loraux) and *Médée* (first performed in 1797, with libretto by François Benoit Hoffmann based on Pierre Corneille and Euripides). The story of the rescue of

Luigi Cherubini, for many years director of the Paris Conservatory, was a leading artist who, besides operas, composed chamber music and religious works (including his *Requiem*, 1816). Ludwig van Beethoven and Johannes Brahms were among his admirers.

Draft of a classical stage set from Antonio Pian and Norbert Bittner for *Medée* (Vienna, 1812).

the girl Lodoïska, who was held prisoner by the demonic knight Dourlinski, became the prototype for the "rescue opera," so popular during the French Revolution; as such, it was also an important source for Beethoven's *Fidelio*. The premiere on July 18, 1791 was much acclaimed, and within a few months hundreds of performances followed both in France and abroad. *Médée* also excited international attention; here Cherubini achieved a hitherto almost unheard transposition into music of psychological events. The overture sounds the mood of French Revolutionary music—another quality it shares with *Fidelio*. Franz Lachner composed an adaptation of this opera in 1855, with through-composed recitatives and an Italian text that turned *Médée* into a *grand opéra*. Nevertheless, after many years of neglect, Lachner's version managed to revive the *Médée* and to establish a place for it in repertoire of many opera houses. Once Maria Callas made the role of Medea her showpiece, the part of Medea has become a kind of touchstone for prima donnas.

Etienne-Nicolas Méhul was, after Cherubini, the most important composer of French operas

François-Adrien Boieldieu, composer of nearly 30 *opéras comiques*, *La dame blanche* (The White Lady, premiered in Paris in 1825, text by Scribe) became world famous. Boieldieu was court composer and director of French operas in St. Petersburg from 1804 to 1811.

Henriette Sontag as Anna in Boieldieu's *La dame blanche* (Vienna, 1826). A celebrated prima donna in Paris and Vienna, Sontag was the first to sing Weber's *Euryanthe*. In later years, she also sang in New York, where operas were eagerly performed decades before the Metropolitan Opera House opened in 1853. Contemporaries praised her clear, true coloratura and the beauty of her appearance.

Daniel François Esprit Auber, composer of about 70 operas, mostly with librettos by Eugène Scribe; in 1842 he became Cherubini's successor as director of the Paris Conservatory.

The singer Révial as Dimitri in Auber's *Lestocq ou L'intrigue et l'amour* (Paris, 1834, text by Scribe).

Giacomo Meyerbeer, born in Berlin as Jakob Meyer Beer, became known through the six Italian operas he wrote after he moved to Italy in 1816. He then accepted an invitation to Paris, where he composed *Robert le diable* (Robert the Devil, premiered in 1831, text by Scribe and Germain Delavigne), his first Grand Opéra. In 1842 he succeeded Spontini in Berlin. With his festival production of *Ein Feldlager in Schlesien* (text by Scribe and Ludwig Rellstab), the Berlin Opera House was reopened—after being destroyed by fire the year before—in 1844.

around 1800. His biblical opera *Joseph* (premiered in 1807 with text by Alexandre Duval) continued the legacy of Gluck in its solemnity. Gasparo Spontini also took up the tradition of Gluck's French operas in his *tragédie lyrique La Vestale* (The Vestal Virgin, premiered in 1807, libretto by Victor Joseph Etienne de Jouy), which anti-cipated the style of *grand opéra* in its blend of Italian *bel canto* and French exactitude, paired with refined instrumentation and opulent staging. The empress Josephine personally patron-ized the production; in 1810 it was awarded as the best opera of the decade, and Spontini's reputation was made. The transition to the *grand opéra* was finally complete with *La Muette de Portici* by Daniel François Esprit Auber (first performed in Paris in 1828). Thanks to the influence of the accomplished dramatist Eugène Scribe, this opera about a mute heroine portrayed by a ballerina, was, in theatrical terms, incredibly effective. Scribe, the Metastasio of the bourgeois age, was the most sought-after dramatist of the French stage in the 19th century. His studio, which employed many authors, produced about 400 plays and librettos. On August 25, 1830, *La Muette* premiered at the opera house in Brussels. The historical subject—a 1647 uprising of Neapolitan fishermen against the Spanish rulers—so inflamed Belgian patriotism among the audience that, before the end of the performance (which was supposed to include a spectacular eruption of Mount Vesuvius as its climax), the spectators streamed out onto the streets crying out for independence from The Netherlands. The revolution took its course; Belgium became an independent nation two months later.

Sophie Loewe as Isabella in Meyerbeer's *Robert le diable* (Vienna, 1833).

In the *grand opéra*, the standard fare of amorous mix-ups are relegated more and more to subplots. Instead, the plot is driven by historical and political events, allowing for effective crowd scenes that demanded large orchestras and elaborate staging. In addition, Meyerbeer's operas required a level of vocal prowess that could only be met by a few exceptional singers—the result ultimately is that his works are rarely performed today.

Jenny Lind, the Swedish soprano, sang Vielka in the premiere of *Ein Feldlager in Schlesien* in Berlin; here she is seen in a revised version of the same piece in Vienna, 1847. In 1849 she retired from the opera stage, performing thereafter only in concerts. In 1850 she toured America, where she gave 150 concerts.

Meyerbeer's *Les Huguenots* (premiered in Paris in 1837, with text by Eugène Scribe and Emile Deschamps) and *Le prophète* (first performed in Paris in 1849, with libretto by Scribe) are based on historical events of the 16th century. The former ends with the murder of the Huguenots on St. Bartholomew's Day; the latter describes the downfall of the Baptists of Münster in the ruins of an exploding castle—scenes of horror that effectively alternate with lyrical episodes and romances typical for French operas. Two interesting facts to note about *Le prophète* for fans of opera history are that the heroine, Fides, written for a deep female voice,

Frieda Hempel as queen in Meyerbeer's *Huguenots*. Born in Leipzig, Hempel became a star at the Met in New York, where she sang from 1912 to 1920.

The alto Pauline Viardot-Garcia sang Fides in the Paris premiere of *Le prophète* and also sang, among other parts, the title part in *Sapho*, Charles Gounod's first opera (Paris, 1851, text by Emile Augier).

became the model for Azucena in Verdi's *Il trovatore* (Troubadour) and, at the premiere, electric light in the form of arc- or carbon light was used for the first time.

Interestingly enough, French opera of the 19th century celebrated its greatest triumph on ground far from the *grand opéra*—in fact, not even in France. Georges Bizet's *Carmen* is an *opéra comique* with a tragic conclusion (premiered in 1875, with libretto by Henri Meilhac and Ludovic Halévy). After its unsuccessful premiere in the *Salle Favart*, Ernest Guiraud supplied recitatives, and in this form, only a few months after Bizet's death, *Carmen* had a brilliant premiere in German in Vienna. Now a *grand opéra*, *Carmen* returned to Paris on its incontestable triumphal march. The realism of the milieu and characters, foreshadowing the later Italian *verismo*, seems all the more remarkable in that the enchanting Spanish local color was caught so vividly by a composer who had never been to Spain.

In France, Richard Wagner was an irritant. He withdrew his *Tannhäuser* after only three performances in Paris as a noisy group hired to clap and disturb successfully sabotaged the

Maria-Felicia Malibran, a mezzo soprano and sister of Pauline Viardot, sang the title character in *Maria Stuarda* by Gaetano Donizetti at its premiere in Milan in 1835.

Anonymous painting of a burning theater—a fate suffered by many theaters as long as open fires were used for stage lighting. Only with the advent of electricity did safe lighting become possible.

The venerable Paris *Académie Royale* went up in flames in 1763; in 1776, the Milan *Teatro Regio Ducale* burned down; in 1817, the Berlin *Schauspielhaus*; the Munich *Nationaltheater* in 1823, barely five years old; in 1843 a fire destroyed the 100-year-old *Oper unter den Linden* in Berlin; in 1836 a fire destroyed the *Teatro La Fenice*, Venice's largest opera house, which had already been rebuilt when a fire burned down the *Teatro San Benedetto* in 1792; Covent Garden, the London opera house, fell victim to fire twice, in 1808 and again in 1856.

The Dresden Opera, built in 1841 by Gottfried Semper, the site of many Wagner premieres, had to move into temporary quarters for nine years after a fire in 1869, until the new opera house, also designed by Semper, could be finished.

In 1881, about 400 people perished in the flames of the *Ringtheater* in Vienna. The cause of the disaster was escaped gas that set the scenery on fire; almost none of the orchestra members survived the disaster. Thereafter, an iron curtain between the stage and the audience was required by law in all large theaters.

Carmen. Draft of a set design by Max Brückner (1880/1881).

Figure of Escamillo (from *Carmen*) by Josef Fenneker (Berlin, 1949)

performance. Nevertheless, the French composers' encounter with Wagner was not without repercussions. Bizet had already, although unjustly, been accused of "wagnérisme," because of his use of leitmotifs, as was Camille Saint-Saëns, who, in spite of his admiration for Wagner, remained a completely independent composer. This is clearly evident in his masterpiece *Samson et Dalila* (premiered in 1877, text by Ferdinand Lemaire), which was originally conceived as an oratorio. Only Ernest Chausson's posthumously premiered *Le Roi Arthus* (first performed in Brussels in 1904 with text by the composer) fell completely under Wagner's influence, although this in no way impairs the quality of this work, which is thematically and musically closer to *Tristan und Isolde* than to *Parsifal*.

Claude Debussy, a friend of Chausson, also started out as a Wagnerian. In *Pelléas et Mélisande*, however (written in 1893 and premiered in 1902), Debussy emerged from

> When so mighty and dominating a genius as Richard Wagner arises in the world, such a light emanates from him that a kind of darkness follows thereafter. Hence, the general uncertainty, the groping attempts in all directions, to evade the overpowering brilliance that seems to block every path.
>
> *Ernest Chausson*

Wagner's shadow and managed to give a new direction to French music. Debussy's art of instrumentation was without equal at that time. His orchestral language transported Wagnerian leitmotifs into a subtle drama of tonal coloration, managing simultaneously to be precise and vague and enfolding the underlying, symbolically enigmatic text by Maurice Maeterlinck with multiple nuances. The vocal passages, flowing with the rhythms of speech, have often been dubbed "unending recitative"—an allusion to Wagner's own "unending melody." Only slightly abridged, otherwise composed true to the text, Debussy's *drame lyrique* became the direct predecessor of the so-called literary opera of the 20th century.

As a reaction against both the content and the formal mixing of *grand opéra* with *opéra comique*, as in *Carmen*, the *opéra bouffe* or operetta came into full flower in the middle of the 19th century.

Many composers were caricatured during their lives, though perhaps none more than Richard Wagner.

Camille Saint-Saëns, misunderstood in his native country as an "incorrigible Wagnerian," was able to produce *Samson and Delila* at the Weimar Hoftheater through the mediation of his friend Franz Liszt. The first performance in France took place 13 years later. As a composer, Saint-Saëns was a master in all genres of instrumental music, as evident in the score to this opera, which is replete with contrapuntal and harmonic artistry.

Claude Debussy followed in the footsteps of Richard Wagner's composed music dramas with their interwoven leitmotifs in *Pelléas et Mélisande*. He avoided, however, Wagner's pathos.

Of this "new old" genre, Jacques Offenbach is the undisputed master, in the tradition of 18th century vaudevilles. Love of mockery and satiric parodies and critiques of contemporary life, packaged in rousing melodies (couplet/chanson), and garnished with dance numbers (cancan), these were the mainstay of Offenbach's theater "Bouffes Parisiens." In the elaborate *opéras féeries* of later years, fantasy and illusions played a central role. Much of this flowed into Offenbach's main work, *Les contes d'Hoffmann* (Tales of Hoff-

Wilhelm Knaack as Hans Styx and Johann Nepomuk Nestroy as Jupiter in a Vienna production of Jacques Offenbach's highly successful "opéra féerie" *Orphée aux enfers* (Orpheus in the Underworld, premiered in Paris in 1858, libretto by Hector Crémieux).

mann, premiered in 1881, with text by Jules Barbier), an opera filled with fantasy, based on motifs from the stories of E. Th. A. Hoffmann.

Tales of Hoffmann, often underrated because of its affinity with operetta, is in fact an attempt to write an opera about opera: During a production of *Don Giovanni*, which renders the frame of the story, three "interludes" take place that, on one level, depict Hoffmann's hallucinations in a Berlin wine cellar, but are, in reality, skillful pastiches of the French, Italian, and German

Tales of Hoffmann: Giulietta's palace in Venice (colored charcoal drawing from 1881, the year of the premiere). At his death, Hoffmann left a nearly finished score of this opera; only the instrumentation needed completion. His friend Ernest Guiraud undertook the necessary elaboration and composed the recitatives, but the so-called Giulietta Act was still missing at the premiere.

operas of the Romantic age. As a whole, they constitute a portrait of the times and its inherent contradictions, which lead to the breakdown of Hoffmann, the romantic artist and drunkard.

Operas of the east

Love of local color, a preference of the 19th century opera world, paved the way for opera exports from countries with no great opera

Tales of Hoffmann: Olympia, the mechanical doll, in Spalanzani's house (Max Bignens, Vienna, 1964).

Modest Mussorgsky aimed in his works to "reproduce simple conversation." He rejected verse forms. The attempt to create living prose set a pattern for 20th-century operas.

tradition. Folklore, so long as it did not strongly affront the listening habits of the audience, became an ingredient for success. The Slavic culture in particular delivered many works that found acceptance outside their country of origin, enriching the international repertoire of "nationalistic operas." In Russia, composers such as Alexey Verstovsky and Mikhail Glinka could overcome the predominance of foreign competitors holding the field since the 18th century. The birth of opera in Russia came in 1836 with the premiere of Glinka's *Shisn sa zarjá* (Life for the Tsar, libretto by Georgi von Rosen). Originally entitled *Ivan Sussanin* after the farmer-hero, a title that appealed to even the 20th century rulers hostile to the tsar, this work has remained steadily in repertoire since its premiere in St. Petersburg, although it has been produced in a variety of politically biased adaptations.

The next generation of Russian composers tried mainly to extricate themselves from dependence on Italian, French, and German operas, a dependence still audible in Glinka. Most successful was Modest Mussorgsky with *Boris Godunov*, which was called a "musical folk drama" when it premiered in St. Petersburg in 1874 (text by the composer, based on a play by Alexander Pushkin), and Alexander Borodin with *Knjaz Igor* (Prince Igor, premiered post-

humously in St. Petersburg in 1890, with a
libretto by the composer). Both works returned
to themes and characters from Russian history
and carried on Glinka's tradition with still
greater emphasis on folkloric elements. Today, it
is generally Nikolai Rimski-Korsakov's arrange-
ments (ridiculed by Igor Stravinsky as "Meyer-
beerization") of these works that are used, which
emphasize their *grand opéra* leanings.

Peter Tchaikovsky's *Ewgeni Onegin* (Eugene
Onegin, first performed in Moscow in 1879,
with text by the composer based on a novel by
Pushkin), on the other hand, takes off in a
completely different direction and orients itself
on the west. Tchaikovsky swore he needed no
"tsars, tsarinas, revolutions, battles, or marches,"
and so composed a bourgeois drama of love,
with each act centered on one of the three lead
characters. This pleasing conception and the
sensitive characterization quickly earned success for *Eugene Onegin* beyond Russia. Artful
characterization also marks the classic drama of
suspense revolving around the secret of an
elderly countess and three playing cards, *Píko-
waja dáma* (The Queen of Spades, premiered in
St. Petersburg in 1890, text by Modest Tchaikovsky, based on a novel by Pushkin), enhanced
with folkloric songs and dances, spunky
elements, and a distinctive rococo-style ballet.

In the Bohemian countries of the Habsburg
empire, the Czech language had a clearly
lower status than German until the year 1897,
although a standard Czech language and
literature had been around for a long time. The
goal of most Czechoslovakian composers was to
create an "appropriate" musical idiom. A

The bass Fyodor
Schaliapin in the role of
Boris Godunov, to which
he gave form more than
any other singer of the
20th century (Vienna,
1927).

Peter Tchaikovsky's
work mediates between
Russian national music,
as propagated by the
Petersburg "Group of
Five" (which included
Mussorgsky, Borodin,
Balakirev, Cui, and
Rimski-Korsakov), and
the Western music
tradition that domin-
ated the Moscow
Conservatory.

competition was held for the best national opera. These efforts culminated in the establishment of the Prague National Theater, which was inaugurated with Bedřich Smetana's *Libuše* (libretto by Josef Wenzig and Ervín Špindler) on June 11, 1881. In *Libuše*, as in Smetana's first opera, which won the aforementioned competition, *Braniboři c Čechnách* (Brandenburgers in Bohemia, premiered in 1866, text by Karel Sabina), the subject matter is historical (*Libuše* is about the myth of the founding of Prague) and its local color is tinged with patriotism. Smetana's *Dalibor* (first performed in 1868, text by Wenzig and Špindler) is similar in its basic plot to Beethoven's *Fidelio*, but unlike most rescue operas, it ends tragically. His best-known work, however, which became world famous after being revised into three acts with through-composed dialogue, was the comic opera, *Prodaná nevěsta* (The Bartered Bride, premiered in 1866, a new version was performed in 1871, with libretto by Karel Sabina).

Smetana's younger compatriot Antonín Dvořák did not confine himself to nationalistic themes in his ten operas. His last two works drew upon the fund of popular operatic material: *Armida* (premiered in 1904, with text by Jaroslav Vrchlicky based on the Italian poet Tasso) was one of the most commonly used opera subjects, while *Rusalka* (premiered in 1901, with libretto by Jaroslav Kvapil based on a folktale) is an adaptation of the "Undine" fairy tale, already popularized through the operas of Hoffmann and Lortzing. Although Dvořák's orchestration did not transcend

Wagner's music dramas, the romantic, magical world of the nymph Rusalka was depicted in the tonal coloring of the *fin de siècle*.

While folklore and modernism were not mutually exclusive for Smetana and Dvořák, in the works of later Czechoslovakian composers their union inspired several fine operas, including Leoš Janáček's *Jenůfa* (first performed in 1904, text by the composer, based on a play by Gabriela Preissová) and the operas of Bohuslav Martinů, *Hlas lesa* (The Voice of the Forest, 1935) and the *Veslohra na moste* (Comedy on the Bridge, 1937), which helped give birth to the short-lived genre of radio opera. Martinů also wrote operas for television, among them *The Wedding* (aired in New York in 1953, with text based on Nikolai Gogol).

Among the Eastern European operas that became a part of the standard international repertoire of the 19th century were *Halka* by Stanisław Moniuszko (1854, new version 1858, text by Włodzimierz Wolski). The wealth of melodies in this work demonstrate why he is often called the "Polish Schubert." Moniuszko was, however, equally skilled in creating effective theater, exploiting expertly the dramatic potential of the fate of the serf Halka who is made pregnant by a nobleman and then shamefully abandoned.

The soprano Rosa Morandi as Rosina in *L'oro non compra amore* by Marcos António da Fonseca Portugal (Paris, 1815). This opera by the Portuguese court conductor and composer premiered in Lisbon in 1804 and was evidence of the still uncontested position of Italian operas in Europe at the beginning of the 19th century. Through the exodus of the entire Portuguese court to Brazil to escape Napoleon, Italian operas suddenly flowered in Rio de Janeiro. Even castrati were imported from Italy. The Portuguese court returned to Europe in 1821, but without the court conductor who became ill and died in Rio de Janeiro in 1830.

Italian opera in the 19th century

Gioacchino Rossini at the age of twenty-nine. When he was 18, Rossini had already pocketed his first opera commission and made so good a job of it that he found himself flooded with work for the next 20 years. The result was about forty operas; then, having become rich, he turned to the art of cooking. "Tournedos Rossini" was his most famous recipe, and except for a few "mistakes" in his old age ("péchés de vieillesse"), he gave up composing.

After the triumph of *L'italiana in Algeri* (Italian in Algiers, first performed in Venice in 1813, libretto by Angelo Anelli), his eleventh opera, Gioacchino Rossini signed a contract with Domenico Barbaia, an opera entrepreneur, who leased San Carlo in Naples, one of the largest and most important opera houses in Italy. Rossini was obliged to compose two operas a year for the impresario, but he was also free to compose for other theaters on the side. He produced operas as an assembly-line worker produced Model T Fords—sometimes with no more than a few weeks between works. Nevertheless, among them are such masterpieces as *Il barbiere di Siviglia* (The Barber of Seville, premiered in Rome in 1816, text by Cesare Sterbini based on Beaumarchais), which, despite its unfortunate premiere, almost effaces the works of Mozart and Paisiello that preceded it. Rossini's enormous output necessitated that he at times used parts of earlier operas in new works. For the *Barber*, he used an overture he had used twice before: first in *Aureliano in Palmira* (Aurelian in Palmyra, Milan, 1813), then in *Elisbetta, regina D'Inghilterra* (Elizabeth, Queen of England, Naples, 1815).

La Cenerentola ossia La bontà in trionfo (Cinderella), based on Charles

The baritone Giorgio Ronconi, Verdi's Nabucco, as the Barber of Seville at the Paris Théâtre Italien.

Perrault's version of the Cinderella story (premiered in Rome in 1817, text by Jacopo Ferretti), was an immediate success, another *dramma giocoso* that catapulted Europe into Rossini fever, although his *seria* and *semiseria* works were received with equal excitement. What makes Rossini's operas—whatever their genre—so exquisite is their catchy but never trite melodies and their rhythmically pleasing orchestration which literally vibrates with energy. Rossini's treatment of vocal parts swings easily back and forth between natural declamation and an almost instrumental artistry, without overtaxing the singers. Rossini countered the singers' customary (over)ornamentation

Giuditta Pasta, one of the queens of bel canto as *Tancredi*. Only Maria Callas, who was often compared to her, reached similar heights of vocal artistry. Both singers also tried to make a comeback after their voices had declined. Pauline Viardot, a contemporary of Pasta, and like her a celebrated prima donna, compared the almost tragic results with the "Last Supper" of Leonardo da Vinci: "The picture is a ruin—but it is the world's greatest painting." Bellini dedicated his *Norma* to Pasta.

(a legacy from the Baroque) by composing exactly what he wanted by way of embellishments. In 1822 he married the Spanish singer

Constanze Tibaldi in the title role of *Tancredi* (Dresden, 1825). Rossini's first *opera seria* (premiered in Venice, 1813, text by Gaetano Rossi, after a tragedy by Voltaire of the same title) offers the alto a beautiful part in the "breeches part" of the hero.

The Austrian tenor Angelo Neumann was as enterprising an impresario as Barbaia. As director of a traveling Richard Wagner Ensemble, which had performed the first *Ring* outside of Bayreuth, he was in great measure responsible for popularizing Wagner's works in Europe.

The sisters Giulia and Giuditta Grisi. The soprano Giulia was engaged as prima donna in both Paris and London, where she was most acclaimed for operas from Donizetti and Bellini. Mezzo soprano Giuditta, the younger sister, sang Romeo at the premiere of *I Capuleti e i Montecchi* (The Capulets and the Montagues), a role that had been composed especially for her by Bellini.

Isabella Colbran, who perfectly mastered his *bel canto* idiom. Her interpretations of the *coloratura* roles in mezzo and alto ranges were so beloved that she contributed in great part to his success, not least in Vienna, where Barbaia took over direction of the *Kärntnertor Theater* and the *Theater an der Wien* in 1821.

After the *Barber*, Rossini never again used the harpsichord-accompanied *recitativo secco*. One of his most important contributions to the development of Italian opera was his ensemble technique, which was both artful and lighthanded, allowing for incredibly turbulent scenes. He also wove the aria and recitative into the complex *scene ed arie*, which overcame the regular alternation of recitative and aria without sacrificing the articulation of action through a series of "numbers." Finally, he decisively influenced the history of the *grand opéra* and elevated the prestige of Italian opera through his *Guillaume Tell* (William Tell, premiered in Paris, 1829, text by Victor

Giulia Grisi as Norma.

Joseph Etienne de Jouy and Hippolyte Louis Florent Bis, after Friedrich Schiller).

William Tell was Rossini's last opera; it inaugurated the great era of "political" operas that would culminate in the work of Giuseppe Verdi and clearly influenced the course of Italian unity (*risorgimento*). The inflammatory content of a *William Tell*—at that time already a classic of world literature—should not be underestimated: Rossini's opera was banned in Vienna at the time of Metternich, and elsewhere could only be performed in censored versions, leading to grotesque "replacements" of the title role with politically acceptable heroes

Gaetano Donizetti was a pupil of the composer Johann Simon Mayr in Bergamo, where music lessons were held under Mayr's direction for talented children of poor parents.

(e.g., "Andreas Hofer" in Berlin and London, "Charles the Bold" in St. Petersburg, and "Rodolfo di Sterlinga" in Rome).

There was nothing new in the use of novels or plays as the basis for operas; what was new was the pace with which opera responded to literary trends. Among the popular subjects of Italian Romantic operas were tales of horror (Gothic novels) or historical novels like those of Walter Scott, one of the most popular authors of the century. Gaetano Donizetti's *Lucia di Lammermoor* (Lucy of Lammermuir, premiered in Naples in 1835, with text by Salvatore Cammarano after Scott), and *Anna Bolena* (written for Giuditta Pasta and premiered at La Scala in Milan, 1830, with text by Felice Romani) are

Fanny Tacchinardi-Persiani, here as Adina in Donizetti's *The Elixir of Love*, also sang the first Lucia di Lammermoor.

among the few of his approximately 30 serious operas that—with the exception of his comic works—are still played in the present day. Of the comic operas—altogether about 40—three still regularly appear in opera repertoire: *L'elisir d'amore* (The Elixir of Love, premiered in Milan in 1832, text by Felice Romani after Eugène Scribe), *La fille du régiment* (The Daughter of the Regiment, first performed in Paris in 1840, text by Jules-Henri Vernoy de Saint-Georges and Jean-François Alfred Bayard), and *Don Pasquale* (premiered in Paris in 1843, libretto by the composer and Giovanni Ruffini, based on a text by Angelo Anelli).

Donizetti's operatic success outshone even that of Rossini, in part because Donizetti wrote "singer operas" par excellence. Probably no more effective vocal part has been written than

Frieda Hempel and Enrico Caruso (right) in Donizetti's *The Elixir of Love* (Berlin, 1910).

the mad scene of *Lucia* (act III), which makes strenuous demands on the soprano's *coloratura* technique, or the extreme range (*tessitura*) of Tonio's cavatina in act I of *The Daughter of the Regiment*, which calls for a high C eight times. Equally brilliant are the ensemble numbers (a skill Donizetti learned from Rossini), for example, in *Don Pasquale*, a work that conveys the spirit of the classical *commedia dell'arte* into the 19th century.

Donizetti's arch rival in the international opera business was the somewhat younger Vincenzo Bellini, another genius of *bel canto*, who, however, wrote no comic operas and unfortunately died young. Of his eleven stage works, four are still often performed today: *I Capuleti e i Montecchi* (The Capulets and the Montagues, first performed in Venice in 1830, text by Felice Romani), *La sonnambula* (The Sleepwalker, premiered in Milan in 1831 with a libretto by Romani, based on a text by Scribe), *Norma* (premiered in Milan in 1831, text by Romani), and *I Puritani* (The Puritans, first performed in Paris in 1835, text by Carlo Pepoli, based on themes from Walter Scott's novel, *Old Morality*). Elvira's mad aria in the *Puritans* served as a direct model for the Lucia aria by his friend and rival Donizetti; Arthur, the leading male role, climbs well over the high C. One admirer of Bellini's elegiac, wide-ranging melodies—the Norma aria "Casta diva" is the most famous—was the young Giuseppe Verdi, who, after the deaths of Bellini and Donizetti, became the leading figure in Italian opera. His unique position in 19th century music history can be compared only with that of Richard Wagner.

Vincenzo Bellini was famous for his sweeping melodies, much admired by Verdi (*"melodie lunghe, lunghe, lunghe"*).

Giuseppe Verdi's rocky but steep, uphill path to success began, as he himself later said, with his third opera, *Nabucco* (premiered in Milan in 1842, with text by Temistocle Solera). Verdi sank into a depression and vowed to give up composing in 1840 after the death of his wife and two children, which was followed, moreover, by the dismal flop of his comic opera *Un giorno di regno* later the same year (premiered in Milan, with text by Felice Romani), *Nabucco* met with the same success as Verdi's first opera *Oberto* (Milan, 1839, with text by Antonio Piazza). It was a phrase in the text of *Nabucco* that turned Verdi away from

As a successful composer, Giuseppe Verdi acquired a large country estate which he managed himself. He liked to refer to himself as a "farmer from Parma," not without pride.

Livia Gerhardt and Wilhelmine Pichl as Julia and Romeo in Bellini's *I Capuleti ed i Montecchi*. Romani, the author of the text, diverged from his source—Shakespeare's *Romeo and Juliet*—by making Tebaldo (Tybalt) not only a political opponent but also Giulietta's bridegroom, to intensify the rivalry between the two young men.

his morose decision and inspired him to compose *Nabucco*: "*Va pensiero, sull'ali dorate*" (Fly, Thought, on Golden Wings). The "Chorus of the Hebrew Slaves," written around this phrase, sung by the Hebrews held by Nabucco/Nebuchadnezzar in Babylon, instantly became the musical standard of the movement to liberate Italy and a secret national anthem. Verdi became a symbolic figure of Italy's *Risorgimento*; his name became thought of as an acronym for the king of Sardinia, the designated head of a unified country: *Vittorio Emmanuele, Rè d'Italia*. "Viva Verdi!" became a political battle cry. The years that led up to the premiere of *Rigoletto* (which opened in Venice in 1851, with

Verdi's Operas

text by Francesco Maria Piave based on Victor Hugo's *Le roi s'amuse*) marked Verdi's first creative period. He occupied himself primarily writing historical operas championing freedom and resisting tyranny. He called this period his "galley years" and wrote more than a dozen operas, with characteristic gripping chorus scenes. His middle period, broken by a number of long interruptions, produced eight operas, starting with *Il Trovatore* (Rome, 1853, text by Salvatore Cammarano and Leone Emanuele Bardare based on a play by Antonio Garcia Gutiérrez) and ending with *Don Carlos* (Paris, 1867, text by François Joseph Méry and Camille du Locle based on a play by the German Romantic dramatist Friedrich Schiller). *Aida* fills something of a transitional position. It was commissioned, for a handsome fee, for the opening of the Suez Canal, and premiered, atypically, in Cairo in 1871 (with text by Antonio Ghislanzoni). Verdi's final creative period yielded two late works that baffled his contemporaries: *Otello* opened in Milan in 1887, *Falstaff* in 1893, both with text by Arrigo Boito

Enrico Caruso as Radames (*Aida*) in Berlin

Arrigo Boito and Giuseppe Verdi, the librettist and composer, respectively, of *Otello* and *Falstaff*, apparently worked well together. Other than da Ponte and Mozart, such congenial teams are uncommon in opera history. Boito himself was a very talented but extremely fastidious composer, though he only completed a single opera, *Mefistofele* (Milan, 1868). His main work, *Nerone*, remained a fragment, though it premiered posthumously under the direction of Arturo Toscanini in Milan in 1924. Boito also distinguished himself through his Italian translations of Richard Wagner's operas, though this was initially a barrier in his relationship with Verdi.

based on plays by William Shakespeare.

The *bel canto* ideal of his predecessors meant little to Verdi. Scenes and arias in the style of Bellini or Donizetti were replaced by more richly structured scenes unbelievably full of contrasts and a level of emotional tension that allowed for no pause in the unfolding of the action. Likewise, the antiquated structure that relied on aria "numbers" fell more and more into disuse in Verdi's middle period. The turning point was actually his *Macbeth* (premiered in Florence in 1847, with a text by Piave based on Shakespeare), Verdi's darkest opera, in which he clearly related Lady Macbeth's sleepwalking scene to common mad scenes but which otherwise had little in common with the works of the so-called *Romanticismo*.

Although Verdi made a half-hearted attempt at "grand opéra" in *Les vêpres siciliennes* (Paris, 1855,

Tito Gobbi, one of Maria Callas's regular partners, as the hero of *Simon Boccanegra* (originally produced in Venice in 1857 with text by Piave; Boito later wrote a new version that was produced in Milan in 1881).

text by Eugène Scribe and Charles Duveyrier), and even in *La forza del destino* (St. Petersburg, 1862, text by Piave), both of which included monumental effects, crowd scenes, and local color, Verdi's ambition really aimed in another direction: His *métier* was clearly the destiny of individuals and differentiated character studies, even of minor characters. His means included his mastery of an orchestral language, including even sometimes shrill tonal effects, and an equally expressive melody line that was inseparable from the words, effectively backed by an unmistakable rhythmic élan pulsing through all his works.

No female singer received higher wages: Adelina Patti was the superstar of Italian opera in the second half of the 19th century. One of her great roles was Violetta in Verdi's *La Traviata* (Venice, 1853, text by Piave after Alexandre Dumas, *fils*).

Adelaide Borghi-Mamo as the gypsy Azucena in *Il Trovatore*.

Francesco Tamagno as Verdi's Otello.

The distillation of all his artistry, filtered down through the Italian and the French opera traditions, is *Otello*, whose full score is surpassed in its complexity and modernism only by *Falstaff*. The latter is an intimate work by comparison, conceived almost as chamber music. At the age of eighty, Verdi, who had not ventured to write a comic work for 50 years, presented the opera world with one of its most precious jewels in this piece about an endearing old scoundrel, based on Shakespeare's *Merry Wives of Windsor* and the second tetralogy on the lives of Kings Henry IV and Henry V. The opera ends with a fugue with a resounding motto encapsulating the wisdom Verdi acquired—perhaps—with age, *"tutto nel mondo è burla:"* everything on earth is fun.

Falstaff cuckolded. Drawing by Lovis Corinth (1918).

Some, like Bellini, want to be melodists; others, like Meyerbeer, want to be harmonists. I don't want to be one or the other. And I want young people, when they begin to compose, never to think of harmonists, melodists, realists or idealists, or futurists, or any of these ridiculous people who adhere to these pedantries. In the hand of the artist, melody and harmony are only a means for creating music, and if some day people stop talking of melody, harmony, of German and Italian schools, of the past and the future, etc. etc. etc., then perhaps we may enter the realm of art.

Giuseppe Verdi, letter dated July 16, 1876

Final curtain call for opera by the "numbers:" Setting out for modern times

On the threshold of the 20th century operas benefited from the accomplishments of Wagner and Verdi but suffered underneath their overriding genius. Not all young composers could escape the pitfalls of artistic epigonism. Richard Strauss, for example, composed his first opera *Guntram* (premiered in Weimar in 1894, with text by Ernst Ludwig von Wolzogen and the composer) as a perfectly Wagnerian work. It was not until he composed his third opera *Salome* that he was able to create his own truly independent work. Other composers who may be considered faithful Wagner disciples are Engelbert Humperdinck in *Hänsel und Gretel* (first performed in Weimar in 1893, text by Adelheid Wette) and Wilhelm Kienzl in the somewhat sentimental opera based on an actual criminal case, *Der Evangelimann* (performed in Berlin in 1895, text by the composer), a work that, though essentially forgotten now, was once as popular as Humperdinck's children's opera remains today.

While composers such as Viktor Nessler (*Der Trompeter von Säckingen*, premiered in Leipzig in 1884, text by Rudolf Bunge based on Viktor von

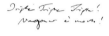

On the day after Wagner's death in Venice (February 13, 1883), Verdi wrote to his publisher Giulio Ricordi: "Sad, sad, sad! Wagner is dead! ... A name that has left an overly powerful imprint on the history of art."

After meeting Engelbert Humperdinck in Italy, Richard Wagner called him to Bayreuth as his assistant in 1880. *Hänsel und Gretel*, his most famous work, continues to dominate the repertory of children's operas; adaptations of Mozart's *Magic Flute* are in second place. The astronomical number of times these two works have been performed is, on the one hand, a nice indication that children's opera is being produced, but on the other hand it suggests the lack of imagination with which producers today are attempting to win the audiences of tomorrow. There are plenty of alternatives: Examples include the children's operas written by Wilfried Hiller (*Der Goggolori*, Munich 1985, text by Michael Ende), *Der 35 Mai oder Konrad reitet in die Südsee* (The 35th of May, or Konrad Rides in the South Sea) by Violetta Dinescu (Mannheim, 1986, text by Florian Zwipf and Ulrike Wendt, based on Erich Kästner), or two modern classics of the genre, *Wir bauen eine Stadt* (We're Building a City) by Paul Hindemith (1931, text by Robert Seitz) and Benjamin Britten's *Let's Make an Opera (The Little Sweep)* (text by Eric Crozier, Aldeburgh, 1949).

Scheffel) or Emil Nikolaus von Reznicek (*Donna Diana*, premiered in Prague in 1894, with text by the composer) followed a pre-Wagnerian Romantic opera tradition, others, such as Karl Goldmark (*Die Königin von Saba*, premiered in Vienna in 1875, text by Salomon H. Mosenthal), followed the example of the brilliant *grand opéra* in the style of Meyerbeer. In Paris, the exotic was back in vogue, as evident in works such as Léo Delibes' *Lakmé* (first performed in 1883, text by

Facing page: "Now I lay me down to sleep, 14 angels watch over me ..." Cloud setting to *Hänsel und Gretel* (Paul Oertel, Kassel, 1895). Originally intended only for home use, ("a dedication play for the nursery"), this fairy-tale opera in three scenes reached the dimensions of half of a Wagnerian music drama after two revisions. Adelheid Wette, the composer's sister, wrote the text based on a story by the Brothers Grimm. Both of the children's parts are usually sung by women, in rare cases by boys. The role of the old witch is often taken by a buffo tenor. The *Sprechgesang* (speechsong) of the third scene became the trademark style of Humperdinck's melodramatic fairy tale *Die Königskinder* (The Royal Children, premiered in Munich in 1897, with libretto by Elsa Bernstein-Porges). It was revised as a complete opera in New York and premiered there in 1910. Humperdinck's approximate speech notations were taken up by Arnold Schönberg (*Pierrot lunaire*, based on poems by Albert Giraud, performed in Berlin in 1912).

Lakmé. Figurine of the Indian goddess Durga (Heinrich Lefler, Berlin, 1906). The name of Delibes became widely known through the doll ballet *Coppélia*, which is thematically related to Offenbach's *Tales of Hoffmann*. In France, *Lakmé* has a fixed place in standard repertory; Lakmé's bell aria in the second act is the most famous part. This was Delibes' last completed opera.

Pierre Edmond Julien Gondinet and Philippe Emile François Gille). It was only in Italy that a group of young composers were able to break through the spell of tradition through their self-determined alliance with contemporary literary works, which allowed them to escape the strictures of verse dramas.

Puccini and *verismo*

Wagner's opera texts were written in alliterative verse, and Verdi, too, continued to use verse form, although the intonation of *Falstaff*—a pleasing *parlando* on the highest musical level—approached the character of free prose. Younger composers, however, were committed to an ideal of a blunt, unadorned naturalism, for which, obviously enough, the use of more formal verse was no longer suitable. Their slogan was *verismo* (from the Italian *vero*, for "true"), and they drew their inspiration from stories like Giovanni Verga's *Cavalleria rusticana*, which also created an uproar when performed as a play. In 1888, Pietro Mascagni composed an opera based on this work in which he used, contrary to the principles of *verismo*, a versified text by Guido Menasci and Giovanni Targioni-Tozzetti. His opera premiered in Rome in 1890.

Mascagni wrote his prize-winning, one-act opera for a composition competition sponsored by the Milan publishing house of Sonzogno to

encourage young
talent and to contract
them to their house.
Both Verdi and the
rising Giacomo
Puccini were under
contract to Son-
zongno's larger
competitor Ricordi, as
was Ruggiero Leon-
cavallo. The latter,
however, was swayed

by Mascagni's success with *I Pagliacci* (first
performed in Milan in 1892, text by the
composer) to leave Ricordi and sign with
Sonzogno. *I Pagliacci* is often performed on the
same program as *Cavalleria rusticana*; both are
key works in the aesthetic transformation then
taking place: In their drastically graphic detail

Adrienne Lecouvreur,
celebrated French
actress at the begin-
ning of the 18th cen-
tury, became the tragic
heroine of a drama by
Eugène Scribe and
Ernest Legouvé. Its plot
is basically true to fact:
Adrienne, the mistress
of the Count of Saxony,
was killed by her rival
by means of a poisoned
bouquet of violets.
Francesco Cilèa trans-
ported *Adriana
Lecouvreur* onto the
opera stage in Milan in
1902, with a libretto by
Arturo Collauti. The
premiere with Angelica
Pandolfini in the title
role and Enrico Caruso
as Count Moritz of
Saxony was a
triumphant success.

Easter Sunday in a Sicilian farming village. Set design by
Ludwig Sievert (Frankfurt am Main, 1931). Before the drama of
jealousy reaches its tragic climax, the *intermezzo sinfonico*,
originally conceived as an entr'acte, is performed. The
premiere of *Cavalleria rusticana* was hailed with sixty curtain
calls. ("Sicilian Peasants' Honor," a translation of the title, is
rarely used today.)

I Pagliacci. The clown of the stage of market fairs, Canio (Bajazzo), became a murderer out of jealousy. Scene drawing by Hein Heckroth, Essen, Germany, 1930. In a prologue, one of the actors explains to the audience that the plot was taken from real life and that his characters are people of flesh and blood. In fact, the story was plagiarized from a French drama, but the play within a play is so cleverly constructed that the audience becomes like one of the actors watching the market comedians and inadvertently witnesses a double murder on the open stage.

In spite of his desire for clarity ("*l'evidenza della situazione*"), Giacomo Puccini tended to be a late Romantic rather than a typical representative of *verismo*. Like Verdi, he used librettos written in verse and closed forms, although he abandoned both the classic "numberical" articulation and the potpourri overtures. Puccini only hinted at the basic mood with a few measures that immediately moved into the first scene; the late Verdi used this technique masterfully in the stormy opening scene of *Otello*.

and in their truthfulness, they fulfill two fundamental demands of literary *verismo*, while remaining true to Verdi's sense of the "melodia italiana."

The preference for the milieu of the common people was characteristic of operas at this time, even in operas that cannot readily be classified as *verismo*, such as *Carmen* or *Der Evangelimann*, though they contain features of *verismo*. Other German and French operas, on the other hand, towed the line of the younger Italians: An example is *Tiefland* (Lowlands) by Eugen d'Albert (first performed in Prague in

1903, with text by Rudolf Lothar based on a play by Angel Guimerà). In this opera, Pedro, a simple shepherd, is called from the loneliness of the mountains into the lowlands to marry the mistress of the unscrupulous landowner Sebastiano, who is in the way of the latter's own marriage plans. When the woman tries to defend herself against Sebastiano's continued and unsolicited advances, Pedro strangles him as though he were a wolf.

Another opera of the "common people" is *Louise* by Gustave Charpentier (premiered in Paris in 1900, text by the composer): The story tells of a Paris working girl in love with an impoverished painter. Despite her parents' disapproval, the desire and enchantment of "free love" prove stronger than filial obedience and middle-class morality.

Charpentier's *"roman musical"* in four acts found its roots in the naturalist literature of the time. Emile Zola, the most prominent exponent of naturalism in France, wrote several librettos for operas by Alfred Bruneau, including *Messidor*, which premiered in Paris in 1897. Bruneau propagated a prosaism of unadorned

Enrico Caruso in a self-caricature as "Julien," in the work following Charpentier's *Louise* (*Julien ou La vie du poète*—Julian, or The Life of the Poet—first performed in Paris in 1913). The tenor to crown all tenors recorded nearly 300 records and became one of the first millionaire recording artists in history. As a lyric-dramatic tenor, he could draw upon an incredible range of repertoire. In the United States—which is where he mainly sang after 1903—he appeared in about forty different roles; the most famous were Canio in *I Pagliacci*, Rodolfo in *La Bohème*, and the Duca di Mantova in *Rigoletto*. Caruso's breakthrough came when he sang the part of Loris in the world premiere of Umberto Giordano's *Fedora* (in Milan, 1898, libretto by Arturo Collauti, after the play of the same name by Victorien Sardou), a *verismo* opera that continued the great success of Giordano's *Andrea Chénier* (premiered in Milan in 1896, text by Luigi Illica also after Sardou) that was also a showpiece role for Caruso.

A caricature of Caruso by Leo Pasetti. Caruso, himself a talented caricaturist, was extremely good humored: When a friend's voice failed him on the stage, Caruso took over the bass role himself.

texts and "people taken from daily life" rather than the "polished figures" of traditional operas.

It was with a story set in the impoverished Parisian artistic, bohemian community of the Latin Quarter that Giacomo Puccini enjoyed his second international success (the first was *Manon Lescaut*, which premiered in Turin in 1893): *La Bohème* premiered four years before Charpentier's *Louise*, in Turin in 1896. The libretto, by Giuseppe Giacosa and Luigi Illica, was based on a novel by Henri Murger, *Scènes de la vie de Bohème* (Scenes from Bohemian Life). After *Manon Lescaut* had surpassed Jules Massenet's own popular *Manon* (1884)—both are based on the novel *L'histoire du Chevalier des Grieux et de Manon Lescaut* by Abbé Prévost— Puccini this time completely outdid his competitor Leoncavallo, who had enjoyed limited success with his own *Bohème* (in Venice in 1897; a second version, *Mimi Pinson*, was presented in Palermo in 1913).

The continuing success and popularity of Puccini's operas from *La Bohème* on is only partly

Café Momus, gathering place for Bohémians. Sketch for a set design by N. Vitalino, Milan, 1910. In fact, there was a café of the same name in the rue de Prêtres in Paris.

explained by his perfect balance between dramatic action and feeling, and between veristic expressiveness and subtle orchestration, which grew increasingly like Wagner's in the instrumentation and in the highly developed use of leitmotifs. The secret of Puccini's success, though, probably lies mostly in his exceptional knack for creating sweet, though never shallow, melodies that seem to charm millions of listeners with the simple enchantment of an addiction.

After *Tosca*, almost a sensational, bloody political thriller (premiered in Rome in 1900, with libretto by Giuseppe Giacosa and Luigi Illica, based on a play of the same name by Sardou), and after the touchingly tender *Madama Butterfly* (Madame Butterfly), interwoven with the sounds of Far Eastern music (*Madame Butterfly* premiered in Milan in 1904; its libretto was the same team who wrote *Tosca*, based on a play by David Belasco and John Luther Long), Puccini composed a

Figurine for *Gianni Schicchi* (Lothar Schenk von Trapp, Darmstadt, 1927). *Gianni Schicchi* was the last of three one-act works by Puccini that opened together under the name *Il trittico* in New York in 1918 (with libretti by Giuseppe Adami and Giovacchino Forzano). The first, *Il tabarro* (The Cloak), a definitely veristic work, describes a gruesome murder committed out of jealousy; the second, *Suor Angelica* (Sister Angelica), takes place in a convent and therefore uses only female voices—an exceptional bit of casting in opera history. *Schicchi*, the third in the trilogy, is a sprightly work about scoundrels performed in parlando style, with great variety in tempo. Here, Puccini pays tribute to the commedia dell'arte and the famed Italian *buffa* tradition.

In 1892, at the age of 25, Arturo Toscanini was already conducting the premiere of *Pagliacci* in Turin. Four years later, he conducted the premiere of *La Bohème* in the same city. At the premiere of *Turandot* at the Milan Scala in 1926, he broke off the performance at the dying scene of Liù in the third act because Puccini had only been able to finish this much of the opera. It was only at the second performance that Toscanini included the final duet and finale of the expanded version. In the early 1930s, Toscanini conducted in Bayreuth, but refused to perform there after 1933 in protest against the Nazi government; he also never performed in Austria after it was annexed by the Third Reich. Toscanini began his career as a cellist; he played in the Scala orchestra at the premiere of *Otello* in 1887.

"western" with a kind of sweeping orchestration. *La Fanciulla del West* (The Girl of the Golden West) was premiered in 1910 at the Metropolitan, with stars such as Emmy Destinn and Enrico Caruso in the lead roles and Arturo Toscanini conducting; its premiere met with tumultuous applause (text by Guelfo Civinini and Carlo Zangarini, based on Belasco). Although *La Fanciulla* did not ultimately prove as popular as Puccini's other operas, it is an important transitional work, leading into Puccini's late style. The happy ending of *La Fanciulla* was unusual for Puccini and may be seen as a concession to American tastes.

Turandot. Sketch of a set design by Franz Karl Delavilla for the German premiere of Busoni's Chinese fable based on Carlo Gozzi (Frankfurt am Main, 1918).

Puccini's last opera, *Turandot*, was left unfinished at the composer's death. It was completed by Franco Alfano from Puccini's notes and premiered after the composer's death in Milan in 1826. The libretto was by Giuseppe Adami and

> My youth was spent in serious study, persistent work and contemplation, nurtured and supported by the German arts and sciences. So only at a relatively late age did I—please forgive me!—come to admire your masterpieces and allow myself to be enchanted by them. *Falstaff* finally brought about in me such a revolution of the spirit and emotions that I can rightfully date a new period of my composing from this point.
> *Letter from Ferruccio Busoni to Giuseppe Verdi, dated 1894 but never sent.*

Renato Simoni after a play by Carlo Gozzi. While the full score does not specifically represent a rejection of harmonious sound and beautiful singing, it does document Puccini's commitment to symphonic construction out of which he developed a work of incredible complexity and exotic tonal color, complete with gongs and Chinese motifs. The overwhelming aria of the Calaf at the beginning of the third act, "Nessun dorma!" seems like a last lingering greeting from the *bel canto* operas of the past.

Inspired by the Roman marionette theater and through an encounter with an Italian comedian, Ferruccio Busoni undertook the musical revival of the *commedia dell'arte*. He composed a two-act *Turandot* that premiered on the same program as his one-act *Arlecchino* (in Zurich, 1917, text by the composer). Busoni used the same fairy-tale material as Puccini in his last opera, but his style and perspective as composer is completely different. His music is ironic and intellectual both in its use of classical elements, as though citing past forms, and in its consciously anachronistic "numberical" structure.

The Goldoni comedies of Ermanno Wolf-Ferrari (for example, *I quattro rusteghi*, The Four Rustics, which was first performed in Munich in 1906, with a libretto by Giuseppe Pizzolato and Luigi Suguna) are only partly comparable to Busoni's

Richard Strauss, one of the last great masters of his trade, was also one of the most commercially successful opera composers.

commedia operas. Wolf-Ferrari plays cleverly with *opera buffa* ensemble techniques, creating such virtuoso curiosities as a "decet" and a tercet for bass voices, elegantly clothed in neo-classicism. In contrast to Busoni—both are German-Italians—Wolf-Ferrari uses quite a small orchestra, about the equivalent of that of Donizetti.

Richard Strauss, on the other hand, wanted far more instrumentalists. Although the late Romantic orchestra had become much larger and much louder, with larger instrumental groupings and additional of new (wind) instruments, Strauss again expanded and demanded orchestras with over 100 musicians.

Strauss and tradition

Strauss and Puccini are the last representatives of a divided opera world. They are the ancestors of Wagner and Verdi, but their paths diverged: Puccini followed almost unswervingly the tradition of the Italian *bel canto*, adapted to suit the changed tonal conceptions of the 20th century, whereas Strauss began as a Wagnerian epigone but, with *Salome* (premiered in Dresden in 1905, with text by Oscar Wilde translated into German by Hedwig Lachmann) and *Elektra* (premiered in Dresden in 1909, with text by Hugo von Hofmannsthal after Sophocles), developed into a late-Romantic Expressionist. In the waltz-happy *Der Rosenkavalier* (The Knight of the Rose, premiered in Dresden in 1911, with a libretto by Hofmannsthal) the pendulum swung back again: The avant-garde, once fortified against strong criticism, gave way to a style of composition that, despite certain tonal excesses, clearly looked more backward than ahead.

Strauss's audience followed his about-faces

faithfully, and all three works became standards in the international opera repertory. Only a handful of composers of the succeeding generations managed to have more than one work performed in the international opera houses. Even Strauss's later works did not match the success of his early work, in part because of the composer's role under Nazism. Although not a member of the National Socialist party, Strauss assumed the office of President of the *Reichmusikkammer* and so became a kind of figurehead for Nazi cultural politics. This move severely undermined his international reputation, even though he gave up the position two years later when he became the target of considerable personal hostility on account of his collaboration with the Jewish writer Stefan Zweig. The immediate cause was *Die Schweigsame Frau* (The Silent Woman), an "opera buffa" based on Elizabethan playwright Ben Jon-

Ariadne auf Naxos. Set design by Hans Schavernoch (Paris, 1983). This one-act work "with prelude" was dedicated to director Max Reinhardt, who founded the Salzburg Festspiele in 1920 with Hugo von Hofmannsthal. Reinhardt directed the original version of this work as an epilogue to Molière's *The Bourgeois Gentleman* for the opening of the Stuttgart opera house in 1912.

Elektra. Draft of a stage design by Emil Rieck for the premiere in Dresden (1909), where most of Strauss's operas had their first performance. With *Elektra*, in which Strauss set to music a tragedy by Hugo von Hofmannsthal that had premiered six years before, a 20-year period of collaboration between the two men began. Hofmannsthal provided Strauss with texts for ten operas. Although he had wanted to turn to more comic subjects after *Salome*, Strauss began with the somber *Elektra* and exceeded his preceding works in harmonic boldness and orchestral force: "Both operas stand alone among my life's works: in them I went to the farthest limits of harmony and psychic polyphony (Clytemnestra's dream) and to the limits of what today's ears can absorb."

son's comedy *Epicoene*. The opera was first performed in Dresden in 1935; Zweig wrote the libretto. Similar in its basic plot to Donizetti's *Don Pasquale*, the piece was immediately stricken from the program after its premiere when Strauss refused to have the Jewish librettist's name removed from the posters.

The names of Strauss's librettists attest to the high literary quality of his operas, especially Hugo von Hofmannsthal, who must be considered an equal partner in the composition of their operas. Together they attained the ideal of a literary opera: The poetry is independent, but in its intention identical to that of the composer. This was not usually the case in other 20th century literary operas. Normally, the music composed was true to the text but at the same time not necessarily in accordance with the author's intentions.

Following upon the nostalgic rococo comedy *Rosenkavalier* (which also ironically paid tribute to the *bel canto* opera in the caricatured minor role of the Singer), Strauss composed *Ariadne auf Naxos* (premiered in Stuttgart in 1912 with a libretto by Hofmannsthal; a new version was produced in Vienna in 1916), a complex "Baroque" opera in which a young composer must watch how a *commedia dell'arte* troupe, engaged by the same impresario, takes over the direction of his heroic opera. Although the orchestra here is reduced to the size of a chamber orchestra, the instrumentation is vibrantly colorful.

Capriccio, which premiered in Munich in 1942 with libretto by Clemens Krauss, is richer than *Ariadne* in tonal color—even "old-fashioned" in its use of the harpsichord—but similar in structure and theme. It is the last of Strauss's 15 operas. The scene is "a castle near Paris, at the time when Gluck began his reform of operas." This "conversation piece for music" treats a question as old as opera itself: Which is more important, the words or the music? Almost two centuries before, Salieri dealt with this problem in an opera parody, *Prima la musica e poi le parole* (First Music, Then Words, first performed in Vienna in 1786, text by Abbé de Casti). Strauss aspires to a kind of synthesis, the quintessence of his 50 years of creative activity in opera, when, at the opening of *Capriccio*, the theater director addresses the audience in words phrased as a kind of slogan: "Give the aria her due! Take the singers into consideration! Not so loud in the orchestra!"

Elektra. Hardly any highly dramatic singer could equal the intensity of the soprano Inge Borkh, who had studied acting at the Max Reinhardt Institute before her debut as Agathe in *Der Freischütz* in Lucerne, Switzerland, in 1940.

Elisabeth Schwarzkopf as Feldmarschallin in Strauss's *Der Rosenkavalier*, in London, 1959. Schwarzkopf also sang this brilliant role in 1960 under the direction of Herbert von Karajan at the opening of the new Salzburg Festspielhaus. With her husband Walter Legge, one of the most influential record producers after the Second World War, she made many recordings. They have remained documents of an exceptionally beautiful and cultivated soprano voice.

Benjamino Gigli
der König der Tenöre
auf Electrola-Musikplatten

Beniamino Gigli, a tenor acclaimed especially for his phenomenal *piano* and *mezzavoce* technique, was considered the rightful successor to Enrico Caruso, who died in 1921. Gigli made his first recordings in 1918. In the 1930s he began a successful film career.

In the history of opera, art and commerce have often gone hand in hand, but it is only since the turn of the 20th century that an entire industry has grown around a form of art. As early as 1906, barely ten years after record production had begun, millions of shellac records had been sold, and in those days the proportion of classical music recordings among the total records sold was much greater than it probably is today. There was a name that went along with this phenomenal success: Enrico Caruso. Caruso's first recordings were made in a hotel room in Milan where he sang ten opera arias with piano accompaniment

in the space of two hours. The producer was Fred Gaisberg of the London Gramophone Company. By the end of his life, the tenor of the century had recorded more than 250 records. One of the female stars of the early years of record production was Nellie Melba, acclaimed worldwide for her *coloratura* soprano; indeed, the ice cream confection "peach melba" was named after her. Equally well known was Emmy Destinn, Caruso's partner in Puccini's *Girl of the Golden West* and other works.

Although the earliest single records offered less than about five minutes of playing time, producers were beginning to make complete opera recordings even in these early days. Cinema, itself in its infancy, also turned to opera as a rich well for material, even before the technology for "talkies" had been developed. Early film versions of operas included *Carmen* (1908) and *Der Trompeter von Säckingen* (1917), shown with obligatory live piano

Bottom, left: Beniamino Gigli in Rome, during the filming of the film operetta, *Dir gehört mein Herz* (Germany/Italy, 1938); behind him (from left): Theo Lingen, Richard Romanowsky, Erich Kestin, and Paul Kemp.

Frieda Hempel
Genossenschaft Deutscher Bühnenangehöriger

Soprano Frieda Hempel, often Caruso's stage partner in Berlin and New York. (Collectors' card photo.)

The birth of a myth: Maria Callas as Isolde in her first engagement at the Teatro La Fenice (Venice, 1947).

Herbert von Karajan
auf der *GRAMMOPHON*
DIE STIMME SEINES HERRN

Herbert von Karajan began his career in 1929 as conductor in Ulm, Germany. In 1935 he became Germany's youngest music director in Aachen. Because he was a member of the National Socialist Party during the Nazi rule, he was temporarily banned from conducting in Germany after the Second World War. In 1946 he made his first record recordings with the London Philharmonia Orchestra, launching an unparalleled recording career.

Maria Callas in conversation with her mentor, the great Italian conductor Tullio Serafin (left) and producer Walter Legge. Callas's recording of Bellini's *Norma* was a high point in classical recording history (Milan, 1954).

Baritone Tito Gobbi celebrated his greatest successes as the title hero of such Verdi operas as *Simone Boccanegra* and *Falstaff*, and also as the sinister Scarpia in Puccini's *Tosca* alongside Maria Callas. His great acting talent could also be admired in the many opera films he made, including *Il barbiere di Siviglia* (1945), *Rigoletto* (1946), ánd a 1964 television production of *Tosca*.

accompaniment. In 1908, the many attempts to combine film and record recordings—beginning with Oskar Messter in 1903—finally achieved some degree of success. The first filmed opera scenes were produced using something called the "needle tone method" to try to match the sound up with the moving pictures; scenes produced in this way included the chorus from *Le prophète* and a duet from *La Bohème*. Around 1919, small opera ensembles began to tour with silent movies, providing live music accompaniment; *The Flying Dutchman* and *Martha* were among the operas performed in this way. At the end of the 1920s, when talkies took hold, film studios liked to hire stars from music halls and operettas; among the performers who got their start in films by this route was Maurice Chevalier. The studios also occasionally

Giuseppe Taddei, next to Gobbi one of the greatest Italian baritones of the postwar years, also made a name for himself as an interpreter of Wagner roles (including Hans Sachs and Holländer, among others).

139

Canadian bass-baritone George London—seen here as Don Giovanni for a Westdeutsche Rundfunk recording (1967)—was among the stars of the Bayreuth Festival in the 1950s and 1960s. London also was acclaimed for his portrayal of the title character in Mussorgsky's *Boris Godunov*.

hired "heavy weights" from the opera stage, like the tenors Leo Slezak or Beniamino Gigli, who managed to make the early transition from stage to movies. These opera singers enjoyed international fame and achieved a kind of star status more common to movie stars today. The opera stage itself also produced many stars who found themselves featured in newsreels and popular magazines and spread their names by performing radio concerts.

Despite periodic dips in the record industry, sales of recordings have basically continued to grow since the inception of the industry, spurred on by technological changes and advances (such as the 33 1/3 rpm LP replacing the 78, the casette replacing the eight-track, and the compact disc replacing the LP).

Enthusiasm for stereophonic high-fidelity reproduction in the 1960s and 1970s brought unprecedented profits to the record industry. Even though the

Italian bass Cesare Siepi in 1972. Siepi's legendary interpretation of Don Giovanni was documented in a film made at the Salzburg Festival in 1953.

proportion of classical music steadily declined compared to the booming pop music, the classi-business nonetheless remained extremely lucrative, especially since only a handful of companies were sharing the world market among themselves.

To this day, the late Austrian conductor Herbert von Karajan (1908–1989) remains an almost guaranteed-to-sell name in classical recordings. Karajan was discovered for records by the producer Walter Legge and would steer the history of the medium more than any other conductor since 1945. Part of his artistic legacy, however controversial they may be, were his opera recordings, which included Mozart's *Marriage of Figaro* with George London as

Soprano Sena Jurinac in 1969; shortly after her debut as Mimi in *La Bohème* in Zagreb, she was engaged by the Vienna State Opera (1944), where she was especially respected as a wonderful singer of Mozart. At the 1960 inauguration of the new Salzburg Festival House, she sang Octavian in *Der Rosenkavalier*. In 1993 she took leave of the stage in the same opera, this time in the role of the Marschallin.

Maria Callas with Giuseppe di Stefano in Berlin during her 1973 concert tour. During the 1950s and 1960s the star tenor di Stefano sang in all the world's great opera houses.

Count Almaviva and Sena Jurinac as Cherubino (1952), Wagner's *Die Meistersinger von Nürnberg* with Theo Adam as Hans Sachs (1971), and a legendary version of Donizetti's *Lucia di Lammermoor* with Maria Callas (1955).

Maria Callas, born of Greek parents and raised in New York City, made her debut in Italy in 1947. After 1951 she sang at the Milan Scala. She began her career with such highly dramatic roles as Wagner's Isolde but her big breakthrough came with a production of Cherubini's *Medea*. She repeatedly proved herself worthy of the throne of a *prima donna assoluta* in such roles as Rosina (*Il barbiere di Siviglia*), Norma, Lady Macbeth, or Tosca, and in her mastery of *coloratura*, as well as in lyrical and dramatic roles. After singing Tosca in London in 1965, she took her leave from the opera stage but still made recordings and even attempted a comeback alongside Giuseppe di Stefano—a humbling experience since both performers were well past their peaks by then. The recordings she made in the 1950s have preserved the wonder of her unique voice and continue to appreciate in value, breaking sales records even

20 years after the primadonna's death.

As the recording industry evolved, it became customary for a vocal artist to sign an exclusive contract with a particular record company. For this reason, many opera recordings have featured less than optimal casts, despite the number of big names participating. The record companies would cast an artist who was already under contract rather than "borrow" a singer from a competitor. These exclusive contracts are no longer financially feasible today, even for the larger record companies. Through multimedia marketing, superstars such as the famous "three tenors" (Luciano Pavarotti, Placido Domingo, and José Carreras) have mined new sources of revenue beyond the imagination of opera singers of the past. Likewise, the world's top orchestras now command incredible fees. An alternative to this upwardly spiralling cost of classical recording is to enlist the cooperation of young, less well known, but artistically promising ensembles. The results are often amazing, particularly in the field of early music, which has from year to year increased its slice of the recording business.

Recent directors of such smaller ensembles have championed a return to the "original sound." Among them are William Christie, who has been a major reviver of the works of Jean-Baptiste Lully, René Jacobs, who has "rediscovered" works of Francesco Cavalli, and the highly regarded Nikolaus Harnoncourt, who has broadened his repertory to include Joseph Haydn and Giuseppe Verdi.

Nikolaus Harnoncourt is one of the most prominent advocates of historically authentic musical performances. His Monteverdi cycle conducted in Zurich with Jean-Pierre Ponnelle as director is considered among the most important opera events of the 1970s.

RODELINDE *Hans Strohbach*

Set design sketch by Hans Strohbach (Berlin, 1924) for *Rodelinde*. In 1920, Oskar Hagen's efforts in Göttingen to revive Handel's operas quickly bore fruit. In addition to the Berlin production of *Rodelinde*, *Julius Caesar* was performed in Cologne in 1924. After the Second World War, two further Handel festivals were established in Germany: one in Halle in 1952, and one in Karlsruhe in 1985. The productions are essentially historical performances using early instruments and leaving room for Baroque improvisation and ornamentation.

Modern Classics

In the 20th century operas have become more and more like museum objects, as it has become harder for new works to gain entrance into stock repertory. New productions of familiar works (whose success is guaranteed) nearly exhaust the available artistic and financial reserves. Only occasionally is there room for something new, but even when a premiere is a success, the final curtain generally falls on the production after only five or six performances. It seems that a repertory of about 200 works is enough to fill the programs of opera houses all over the world, so there is hardly any demand for new productions; indeed, the taste for "discoveries" is often satisfied with "rediscoveries," as the growing interest in operas by Handel and by Monteverdi proves.

Even works of the early 20th century, once almost forgotten, are being rediscovered and have attained the status of classics—as well-tried stand-ins for a so-called modern program. A mere glance at the statistics of opera houses makes the point: Among the twenty most performed works in Germany, for example, first on the list is always Mozart's *Magic Flute*, and the only 20th-century operas included are those of Puccini and Strauss. Far behind and only cropping up sporadically are works like Alban Berg's *Wozzeck* (which premiered in Berlin in 1925, with text by the composer based on *Woyzeck*, a dramatic fragment by the 19th century German playwright Georg Büchner) or Paul Hindemith's *Cardillac* (premiered in Dresden in 1926, with text by Ferdinand Lion based on the novel *Das Fräulein von Scudéri* by E.Th.A. Hoffmann). Admittedly, there are great variations from country to country: The "standard repertoire" in Moscow is different from that in New York. Nonetheless, it is generally fair to say that the repertory is fixed and consists predominantly of 19th century works.

Die tote Stadt (The Dead City), by Erich Wolfgang Korngold (drawing of a set design by Ludwig Sievert, Frankfurt, 1921). Korngold's most famous work, first performed in Hamburg and Cologne in 1920, with text by the composer, is based on the symbolist novel *Bruges-la-morte* by Georges Rodenbach. Korngold was a mere twenty-three years old when he composed it. Within a short time, this theatrically effective, brilliant opera that is strikingly orchestrated and moves between dream world and reality, was performed at all the large German theaters. In 1934 Korngold followed the director Max Reinhardt into exile in the United States, where they were working on a movie version of Shakespeare's *Midsummer Night's Dream*. Korngold went on to become one of the most successful composers in Hollywood.

Wozzeck in the doctor's office; the doctor misuses him as a guinea pig (picture of a scene by Eduard Löffler, Mannheim, 1932). The story of the murderer who killed out of jealousy would have been material for a *verismo* opera, but Berg shapes it into something completely different: a fifteen-part series of scenes of suffocating intensity, musically bound to a highly artificial structural concept, in which the forms (passacaglia, fugue, rondo, etc.) are meant to remain hidden from the listener. The mainly atonal music, filled with daily sounds (military band, folk songs), illuminates the abyss of human existence while silent cries of a broken soul grow loud, as if echoing the hopelessness of the catastrophe of the First World War.

Wozzeck is a key work of the modern period. It gave the ever more influential Schönberg school (centered on the atonal expressionism of Arnold Schönberg), to which Berg belonged, the attention and respect of a large public, more than Schönberg's own short operas or melodramas could (these hardly aroused interest outside of certain knowledgeable artistic circles). Schönberg's *Erwartung* (Exüectation), which he wrote in 1909, premiered in Prague in 1924 with text by Marie Pappenheim; *Die glückliche Hand* he wrote in 1913; he also wrote the libretto. It premiered in Vienna in 1924. Both operas were more like musical-scenic "snapshots"—fleeting depictions of puzzling interior worlds, inspired or at least indirectly influenced by Sigmund Freud's theory of psychoanalysis. In many ways these works were signs of future trends—the use of rhythmic declamation in *Pierrot Lunaire* and in Berg's own *Wozzeck*, the spoken choruses of *Die Glückliche Hand*, the attempt to "make music" via theatrical means (light crescendo), an idea picked up again in modern music theater conceptions, as in Mauricio Kagel's "instrumental theater."

Cardillac: set by Ludwig Sievert (Frankfurt, 1928): Anyone who bought a jewel from the sinister goldsmith had to pay for it with his life. Hindemith's first full-length opera mirrored a tendency toward a new realism, countering the pathos-imbued operas of the late Romantic era. Characteristic of these works is the inde-pendent orchestral part, which approaches pure instrumental music.

A number of composers attempted to strike a balance between the late romantic and the avant-garde, keeping equally distant from both. An example is Franz Schreker. In the early part of the 20th century, Schreker was as famous as Richard Strauss and Arnold Schönberg and considered one of the leading artists of German-Austrian

Paul Hindemith as conductor. At the 1921 Stuttgart premiere of his expressionist one-act works, *Mörder, Hoffnung der Frauen* (Murder, Hope of Women, with text by Oskar Kokoschka) and *Das Nusch-Nuschi* (text by Franz Blei), he prompted a huge theatrical uproar. Large segments of the audience were outraged by the scarcely veiled depiction of violence and sexuality. His third single-act opera, *Sancta Susanna*, performed a year later in Frankfurt, managed to affront religious sentiments. An aria about the advantages of the availability of hot water, performed in a hotel bathtub (*Neues vom Tage*, Berlin, 1929, text by Marcellus Schiffer) also caused a hue and cry. It was not until the Nazis came to power, however, that his works were actually banned, since the Nazi government took it upon itself to act as guardian of people's sensibilities. Under increasing pressure, Hindemith came to the United States in 1940 and was a highly esteemed Professor of Music at Yale until 1953. After he returned to Europe, he wrote *Die Harmonie der Welt* (The Harmony of the World, premiered in Munich in 1957), an opera about astronomer Johannes Kepler. This work was, however, overshadowed in the postwar German opera world by his own *Mathis der Maler* (Mathis the Painter), which, condemned by the Nazis and therefore premiered in Zurich 1938, was not heard in his native country until after the war. The conductor Wilhelm Furtwängler, who had used his influence to have it performed in Berlin in 1934, resigned all his posts in protest against the ban on *Mathis*.

Screen projection by Teo Otto for a 1957 Hamburg production of Alban Berg's *Lulu*. *Lulu*, Berg's second opera, was never completed. The premiere of the fragment, with text by the composer based on the tragedies *Erdgeist* (Earth Spirit) and *Die Büchse der Pandora* (Pandora's Box) by Frank Wedekind, took place in Zurich in 1937, two years after the composer's death. A full version of this work was finally performed in Paris in 1979: Friedrich Cerha finished the opera using the original composer's notes to the third act that had not been made available for a long time.

avant-garde in music. His works were very successful but were banned in Germany after 1933, as the Third Reich purged him from the cultural mainstream on the double grounds of being Jewish and homosexual. Since the end of the 1970s, his operas, including *Der ferne Klang* (The Distant Sound, premiered in Frankfurt in 1912) and *Die Gezeichneten* (The Branded Ones, also premiered in Frankfurt, in 1918) have received something of a second life.

Schreker wrote his own librettos and had a predilection for scenes filled with erotic tension, which he set to music with a tonal sensuousness that is almost impressionistic. Musically comparable was the composer Riccardo Zandonai, whose tonally enchanting *Francesca da Rimini* (premiered in Turin, 1914, with text by Tito Ricordi, based on the tragedy of the same name by the Italian poet Gabriele D'Annunzio) is all the more lovely as Zandonai enriched the tonal coloring of the orchestra to include such old instruments as the lute and the viola pomposa.

From Strauss's *Salome* , with its dance of the veils to Berg's *Lulu*, eroticism became a regular component of early 20th century operas. Even in Maurice Ravel's *buffo*-like one-act *L'heure espagnole* (Spanish Time, written in 1907 and premiered in Paris in 1911 with libretto by Franc-Nohain [Maurice-Etienne Legrand]), eroticism propels the action forward. Although originally decried as a "pornographic operetta," this uninhibited description of lover's private hours quickly gained international acceptance. The music, imbued with Spanish local color, cleverly draws the scene of action, a watchmaker's shop, into the tonal setting.

Béla Bartók's one-act fairy tale *Blue Beard's Castle* (premiered in Budapest in 1918, with text by Béla Balász [Herbert Bauer]), demonstrated the self-destructive potential of the sexual tension between man and woman. This is an epochal work in its tonal symbolism and its rich dissonance, which makes it all the more articulate. Bartók's typical wealth of rhythmic structures is even more

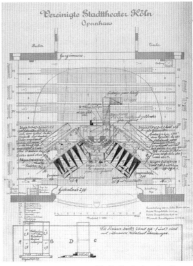

Technical plan by Hans Strohbach for *Blue Beard's Castle*. The carefully directed and produced 1926 performance in Cologne was overshadowed by the premiere of the ballet-pantomime *The Miraculous Mandarin* at the same evening. Even after the dress rehearsal, national-conservative circles had launched a campaign against this "whorish work." Without having seen the work, Konrad Adenauer, then mayor of Cologne, immediately ordered that it be stricken from the program—a unique procedure in the theater history of the 1920s.

Jonny spielt auf (Jonny Strikes Up), by Ernst Křenek (Leipzig, 1927, text by the composer). Drawing of a set design by Johannes Schröder (Duisburg, 1928). Křenek's sensationally successful opera was immediately taken over and performed on many stages after its premiere and stirred strong reaction everywhere. Křenek became the target of overt racial abuse; in Vienna the National-Socialist party organized protests against the "Jewish-Negroid sullying" of the Staatsoper.

Jonny spielt auf. Draft of a poster as stage decoration (Lothar Schenk von Trapp, Darmstadt 1928). Křenek's work was a classic example of a contemporary opera in the rhythm of the modern metropolis. Jonny, a black jazz violinist and a thief who steals instruments, embodies the spirit of the times. Max, on the other hand, the brooding composer, must learn that the Romantic era is over.

evident in the ballet-pantomime *The Miraculous Mandarin* (premiered in Cologne in 1926, based on a text by Melchior Lengyel).

In Russia in 1917, the outbreak of the October Revolution drove many Russian artists into exile. Among them, Sergei Prokofiev left his home and emigrated to the United States for some time. In Chicago he saw the premiere of his burlesque piece, *L'amour des trois oranges* (The Love of Three Oranges, with text by composer, based on a 1761 play by Italian dramatist Carlo Gozzi), in 1921. Inspired by the *commedia dell'arte* and full of opera parody, Prokofiev's work plays with anti-illusionistic tendencies, setting up rivaling "audience" choruses to comment on the action. Through the efforts of director Vsevolod Meyerhold, who first introduced Prokofiev to the subject matter, this

Maschinist Hopkins (Duisburg, 1929) by Max Brand. Set design by Johannes Schröder for the premiere. Brand, who like his teacher Schreker also wrote his own texts, promoted stylistic pluralism. This opera, a socially critical work in the working-class milieu, combines influences from the Schönberg school (twelve-tone technique, *sprechgesang*), sound effects (machine music), and jazz elements in an almost movie-like montage technique that became the basis for the style of George Antheil's *Transatlantic* (Frankfurt, 1930, text by the composer). The American composer Antheil actually included film and screen projections in the plot and expanded—as has been done in his *Ballet mécanique* in 1925—the range of sounds through mechanical and electroacoustic noises (typewriter, telephone).

Conductor Otto Klemperer. Sketch by Otto Dix (1923). After six successful years in Cologne, Klemperer moved on to Berlin, where under his leadership the Kroll-Opera became the most famous venue for avant-garde productions. Hindemith's *Neues vom Tage* and Stravinsky's staged oratorio *Oedipus Rex* (1928, concert version premiered in Paris in 1927, text by Jean Cocteau) were first produced here. In 1931, however, political pressure closed the opera house, and in 1933 Klemperer was forced into exile. In the U.S. he conducted the Los Angeles Philharmonic Orchestra, the New York Philharmonic, and the Philadelphia Orchestra, then became principal conductor for the Philharmonic Orchestra in London.

opera anticipates the epic theater, which was to become so important in the works of Bertolt Brecht and Kurt Weill, *Die Dreigroschenoper* (The Threepenny Opera, 1928) and *Aufstieg und Fall der Stadt Mahagonny* (The Rise and Fall of the City of Mahagonny, 1930). In Dmitri Shostakovich's opera *Nos* (The Nose, premiered in Leningrad, 1930, with text by Georgi Jonin, Arkadi Preiss, Yevgeny Samiatin and the composer), the alienation effect, central to Brecht's guiding theory of theater (whereby the German playwright called for certain mechanical and literary devices to keep the audience ever aware that they are watching a spectacle and to forestall their being drawn in emotionally), became the most important element of style on a purely musical level. This brilliantly adapted satire based on a short story by 19th century Russian author Nikolai Gogol, in which a lost nose suddenly reappears "in the form of a city councilor," provoked suspicion among high-ranking state officials and disappeared from opera programs shortly after its premiere. Shostakovich's second and last surviving opera did not fare any better: *Ledi Makbet Mzesnkogo ujesda* (Lady Macbeth of Mzesnk, first performed in Leningrad in 1934, with text by Alexander Preiss and the composer, based on a story by Nikolai Leskov) could only be heard again 30 years after its premiere in a "politically correct" new version as *Katarina Ismailova* (Moscow, 1963).

Igor Stravinsky was the undisputed leader of the Eastern European avant-garde, which not only influenced opera but also caused a sensation in Western dance. Stravinsky's Paris premieres were counted among the most spectacular theatrical events of the years from 1910 *L'oiseau de feu* (The Firebird) to 1920 (*Pulcinella*), culminating in the controversial and, some felt, scandalous *Le sacre du printemps* (The Rite of Spring, 1913). After *Le Rossignol* (The Nightingale, Paris, 1914, text by the composer and Stepan Mitusov based on a tale by Hans Christian Andersen), Stravinsky again turned to opera during the 1920s: The cheerful one-act *Mavra* (premiered in Paris in 1922, text by Boris Kochno) was a homage to Russian author Alexander Pushkin, and composers Mikhail Glinka and Peter Ilyich Tchaikovsky, as well as to the

Kurt Weill in the year the songspiel *Mahagonny* was premiered (Baden-Baden, 1927). The former pupil of Humperdinck and Busoni met playwright Bertolt Brecht in the mid-1920s, and Brecht allowed him to set his *Mahagonny* songs to music. The resulting songspiel was a great success, though it was surpassed by the triumph of the same authors' *Threepenny Opera* the following year (Berlin, 1928). The extent of Brecht's contribution to this work is still a matter of debate. Although he signed as author and claimed the lion's share of the royalties, arguments claiming his colleague Elisabeth Hauptmann as author carry some weight. It was Hauptmann who rediscovered Gay/Pepusch's 1728 operetta *The Beggar's Opera*, translated the classic into German, and showed it to Brecht once it had already been put into a form suitable for the stage. Since the street-ballad-like songs do not demand highly developed vocal skills, though the piece does demand talented actors, *Threepenny Opera* is usually considered a play rather than an opera. On the other hand, *Aufstieg und Fall der Stadt Mahagonny* (The Rise and Fall of the City of Mahagonny, Leipzig, 1930), the three-act version of Brecht and Weill's original songspiel, does demand the full-scale facilities and personnel of an opera house: Just this once, Weill was able to realize his ambition to write a "real" opera, despite Brecht's opposition. The tumultuous premiere was followed by several other productions through 1931, but all were accompanied by protests against this anticapitalist "propaganda piece."

Walter Felsenstein. Drawing by Otto Pankok. As a director, Felsenstein was a member of a relatively young profession. In the Baroque era, direction was handled by theater architects and engineers while the ballet masters were responsible for choreography. In the 19th century, both conductors and composers handled the direction at least in part. A perfect example is Richard Wagner, who directed his own works. The idea of a director as an independent profession, an artist who creates something personal out of a text and a full score, only arose at the turn of the century, after theater practitioners and theoreticians like Adolphe Appia and Edward Gordon Craig sounded the knell for the end of the illusionary stage. The peepshow-style stage became the arena where the creative fantasy could develop freely. Felsenstein tried to import into his opera work Constantin Stanislavsky's ideal of realistic acting. Singing is understood as a "dramatic condition;" opera is equated with "music theater." A number of contemporary opera directors consider Felsenstein their mentor. Among his most famous productions at the Komische Oper in Berlin are *Orpheus in the Underworld* (1948), *Othello* (1959), and *Carmen* (1949, 1972).

Italian *opera buffa*. In its West-East synthesis, it is a typical Stravinsky work. It also marked the beginning of the composer's neoclassic period of activity, which lasted nearly thirty years and again culminated in an opera, *The Rake's Progress*, which was first performed in Venice in 1951 (the text is by the poet W. H. Auden and Chester Kallman, based on a series of paintings by English artist William Hogarth).

Stravinsky's ironic stylistic paraphrase of a classical opera, including *recitativo secco* and moralistic warnings—it could have been subtitled, like Mozart's *Don Giovanni*, "the justly punished scoundrel"—was, on the one hand, an attempt to make tradition useful but, on the other, an attempt to distance himself from it. Despite the great success of this opera, Stravinsky seems to have found this road a dead end. In the 1950s he radically changed direction, moving in the direction of the chromatic twelve-tone technique of Schönberg.

As a citizen of the world, Stravinsky espoused a stylistic pluralism, a sign of the declining interest in the tradition of nationalistic operas during the 20th century. But nationalism was not yet completely obsolete. In *Ero s onoga svijeta* by Jakov Gotovac (Ero the Joker, premiered in Zagreb in 1935, text by Milan Begovic), a Croatian work entered the international scene. Bavaria, too, took its turn with *Die Bernauerin* by Carl Orff (opened in Munich in 1947, with text by the composer). Strictly speaking, this is not so much an opera as a melodramatic piece in local dialect with only one song (song of the Italian minstrel); still, the musicality of the strong old-Bavarian dialect, echoed in the opulent, full orchestra, is noteworthy. Another modern composer, Werner Egk based many of the themes in his fairy-tale opera *Die Zaubergeige* (The Magic Fiddle, premiered in Frankfurt in 1935, text by Ludwig Andersen [Ludwig Strecker], based on Franz Graf von Pocci) on Bavarian folk music, which in its moderately modern, occasionally bitonal harmonic accents, just barely met the German standard of the politically acceptable.

Porgy, the destitute cripple in his goat cart (final scene in the staging of the premiere, with the bass baritone Robert Todd Duncan in the title role). *Porgy and Bess* has many *verismo* features, including realistic depiction of the milieu of common people and a text that strives for a natural intonation, close to dialect. Gershwin spent some time in Charleston, South Carolina, where the action takes place, in order to study the music and speech of the black population. In Los Angeles, his actual home, he befriended his neighbor Arnold Schönberg, who had been driven out of Berlin by the Nazis.

Igor Stravinsky's creative period spanned more than half a century and included all genres of vocal and instrumental music of the 20th century. After moving from France to America at the outbreak of World War II, Stravinsky lived in Hollywood where he became an American citizen in 1945. It wasn't until 1951, in order to direct the premiere in Venice of *The Rake's Progress*, that he finally visited Europe again. This work is a fundamental one of the modern opera canon, in part because of the excellent libretto by Auden and Kallman, who also wrote for Hans Werner Henze. "No good opera plot can be reasonable," said Auden (a Pulitzer-Prize-winning poet), "for when people are reasonable, they do not sing."

In *Porgy and Bess*, which opened in New York in 1935 (with text by Du Bose Heyward and Ira Gershwin), George Gershwin succeeded in writing an opera with a "folksy" subject matter whose music was so close to folk melodies that the opera seems idiomatic. Although the music actually was the original work of the composer, to millions of listeners songs like "Summertime" seemed like pop hits or jazz standards, not operatic arias. Radio, recordings, and a movie version made by Otto Preminger (1950) helped make *Porgy and Bess* one of the most famous operas of the 20th century and, due to this multimedia publicity, also one of the most financially successful. Nonetheless, it took some time for the opera's supporters to overcome the deeply held prejudices against a work that not only portrayed blacks but also was cast with black performers; in the 1920s black roles (such as Othello) were generally played by white actors in blackface or masks. In 1955 the alto Marian Anderson became the first black artist to sing at the Met, more than seventy years after New York's Metropolitan Opera had opened. Gershwin, however, expressly demanded a black ensemble. Therefore *Porgy*, even though performed for many years in Europe, was mainly staged by traveling American troupes.

Conductor Ferenc Fricsay. At the premiere of *Danton's Death*, Fricsay took over for Otto Klemperer, who was ill. The highly acclaimed premiere in Salzburg launched a great career that unfortunately ended abruptly with Fricsay's untimely death in 1963. This study of a conductor shows Fricsay in the 1950s in West Berlin.

Between anti-opera and neo-Romantic: The music theater redefines itself

To the composers who survived the Second World War and the devastating purges under Nazism, it became clear that much of what opera had been was buried under the annihilation machinery of the Third Reich. The period of musical quietus, moreover, was not confined to Germany, and it was followed by a certain disorientation among artists. This was overcome by the younger generation of composers only through the constructive debate with the Schönberg school. Twelve-tone theory and the concept of serial music derived therefrom, was the key to a new beginning, which opposed moderate modernism as strongly as the worn-out traditions of late romanticism. In addition, the artistic avant-garde steered clear of traditional opera, finding smaller forms and smaller-scale productions more flexible and therefore more suited to experimentation. So it was left to the generation between the wars and to older composers such as Hindemith, Egk, and Orff to compose new works for the opera.

At the Salzburg Festival in 1947, Gottfried von Einem drew attention to himself with his revolution drama *Dantons Tod* (Danton's Death), based on a play by Georg Büchner. The composer co-wrote the libretto with Boris Blacher. This opera holds on to tonal harmony and formal

Moses und Aron. Drawing of a set design by Achim Freyer (Cologne, 1978).

When he was nearly 60 years old, Schönberg found his way back to his Jewish faith. His last opera is the result of many years of religious questioning. Begun in the 1930s, the composition is based on plans for a cantata, or an oratorio, which explains why the chorus has so large a part in the opera. After the first two acts were completed, years passed before Schoenberg took up the third. Nevertheless, it remained incomplete, except for the text and some sketches. The dramatic premiere of the first two acts took place in Zurich in 1957, six years after Schönberg's death; two years later in Berlin the third act was added for the first time by using the music from the first act to support the spoken text. Moses, a speaking role (with approximate notation as to the height of the tone), symbolizes abstraction and "pure teaching," whereas Aron, a tenor role, embodies the sensible world of feeling. It seems legitimate to infer herein a symbol for the polarity inherent in creative activity, which, in fact, Schönberg himself experienced as a duality.

Benjamin Britten, after Richard Strauss and Puccini, is the most-performed opera composer of the 20th century. For a long time at the periphery of the musical development in Europe, Great Britain entered the international opera world with brilliance in the person of Benjamin Britten. *Peter Grimes* (London, 1945, text by Montagu Slater) was Britten's first opera. It was immediately successful and was performed abroad on a number of stages. In fact, Britten's chain of successes remained unbroken through his last opera, *Death in Venice* (Aldeburgh, 1973, with text by Myfanwy Piper based on a novella by Thomas Mann). Only the pompous work *Gloriana* (London, 1953, text by William Plomer), commissioned for the coronation of Queen Elizabeth II, failed to please, probably because the character of Elizabeth I displays such unpleasant qualities as cruelty and vanity. Public enthusiasm for *A Midsummer Night's Dream* (Aldeburgh, 1960, text by Peter Pears and the composer based on Shakespeare) was unanimous. Here, Britten made the Shakespearean world accessible to contemporary life. The highly effective orchestration describes each of the three planes of action as specific tonal spheres; "very British" is the role of the fairy king Oberon as a countertenor while the performance of the play by the rustics in the third act is an intelligent parody of Italian opera.

articulation through vocal "numbers." The melodic line of the title role is sharply contrasted against the aggressive, noisy chorus scenes of the Parisian crowds.

Wolfgang Fortner, like von Einem, was also not a proponent of the young avant-garde, although he studied the Schönberg twelve-tone technique after the war and was thereby able to avoid the strictures of neo-classicism. His *Bluthochzeit* (Blood Wedding), a literary opera based on a play by the Spanish poet and dramatist Federico García Lorca (premiered in Cologne in 1957, with verse by Enrique Beck), is founded on the conviction "that the renewal of music theater ... can only be brought about through the musician's mastery of play-acting." Hans Werner Henze, a student of Fortner, continued undeterred on this path. His "spoken opera" *Das Wundertheater* (premiered in Heidelberg in 1949, with a text by the composer based on Miguel Cervantes) was the first in a series of works for the stage that includes until today more than twenty pieces for ballet and opera.

Henze's *Boulevard Solitude* (premiered in Hannover in 1952, text by Grete Weil) is a contemporary version of the 18th-century French novel by Abbé Prévost, *Manon Lescaut*. In it, Henze interrupts serial compositional sequences with quotations from Puccini and jazz, expressing his skepticism toward his colleagues and their constructivist aestheticism, which he finds comparable to the "dryness of algebra." *Der junge Lord* (The Young Lord, premiered in Berlin in 1965, with text by Ingeborg Bachmann based on a tale by Wilhelm Hauff) is a comedy without a happy ending. Here Henze temporarily revived the ensemble opera and tonality of Mozart and Rossini. *Die Bassariden* (The Bassarids, first performed in Salzburg, in 1966, with a text by W.H. Auden and Chester Kallman based on Euripides) revived the *opera seria*, although only tentatively, using highly romantic instrumentation and a kaleidoscopic mixture of styles from different epochs. Nevertheless, the opera includes an intermezzo inserted in the form of a Baroque pastoral.

Where Henze staunchly held fast to a certain conventionally plot-structured opera and, until the end of the 1960s, articulated political opinions only with great reservation, Italian composer Luigi Nono exploded the conventions of classical drama and dived into political foment with *Intolleranza 1960* (first performed in Venice in 1961, text by Angelo Maria Ripellino, using texts from a variety of authors including Brecht, Mayakovsky, Sartre, and others). The protagonists

Bernd Alois Zimmermann in the year his most important work was premiered: *Die Soldaten* (The Soldiers, Cologne, 1965, text by the composer based on a play by Jakob Michael Reinhold Lenz). Zimmermann's full score was initially rejected as unplayable, but in fact it guided the relentless serialism of the postwar avant-garde, to which Zimmermann felt himself partly drawn, in a direction more at home with the music tradition. Through the simultaneous depiction of different levels of time and action, the deployment of multi-media (film projections, tapes) and collage techniques (Gregorian chants, Bach chorales, jazz), the structure of the work seems continuously in danger of falling apart. But the danger is averted and the work buttressed through the strict arrangement of the material. The titles of scenes, reminiscent of Berg's *Wozzeck* (ciacona, toccata, rondino, etc.) describe the character of the movement rather than an actual formal structure. The three classical unities—action, time, and place—which had already been repudiated by Lenz, are also dismissed by Zimmermann: "Future, present and past are exchangeable," he said, and clothed this thought in the metaphor of the "circularity of time." *Die Soldaten* is considered by many the "opera of the century," one of the most important works of the postwar years.

are nameless, interchangeable, like the images of modern terror, in this desolate collage: oppression, torture, concentration camp imprisonment, environmental catastrophes pervade the scenes; nevertheless, something like hope sounds in the final chorus. Although at first sight *Intolleranza 1960* appears quite unusual, it actually had predecessors in the opera tradition of the early 20th century, as evident from comparison with Schönberg's melodramas and Leoš Janáček's *Z mrtvého domu* (From the House of the Dead), which premiered in Brünn in 1930, after the composer's death (text by the composer based on the novella by Fyodor Dostoyevsky). The latter opera proceeds like a documentary, portraying a sequence of scenes from a Siberian prison.

Another tradition that grew out of the 1920s, originally in France and continuing today, adopted ancient stories and personages; an example is Arthur Honegger's *Antigone* (premiered in Brussels in 1927, text by Jean Cocteau). Another, Luigi Dallapiccola's *Ulisse* (premiered in Berlin in 1968, with text by the composer using texts by a variety of authors), is a late work that the author himself regarded as "*Il risultato di tutta la mia vita*"—the result of my entire life—though it may also be seen as a preliminary summation of a century, insofar as it incorporates the three basic directions of modern opera: literary standards, structure, and last but not least, Italian cantability.

Argentinian composer Mauricio Kagel took the first step in the direction of anti-opera in *Sur scène* (first performed in Bremen in 1962), a "chamber musical theater piece" for three instrumentalists and three actors—a music professor who speaks disjointedly, and a mime and a singer,

Bernd Alois Zimmermann's *Die Soldaten*, piano version, page 534: In the upper system are notations for "attacking low flying planes;" underneath are "military commands."

161

who imitate each other. The concept was enlarged into Kagel's *Staatstheater* (premiered in Hamburg in 1971), in which nine independent opera plots like "Contra Dances" (a ballet for non-dancers) or "Ensemble" (for sixteen voices) can be combined with one another in almost any order; the only imperative is creative choice, as the sum of all the single actions takes longer than the obligatory prescribed duration of 100 minutes.

Hungarian composer György Ligeti's *Le Grand Macabre* (premiered in Stockholm in 1978, text by Michael Meschke and the composer after a play by Belgian dramatist Michel de Ghelderode), can be seen as an anti-anti-opera, a deliberately simple drama, reminiscent of medieval market fair plays. Ligeti's orchestral spectrum ranges from the harpsichord to the electric doorbell, from the saucepan to the kazoo, producing an arsenal of sounds particularly for purposes of parody: even car horns blow a *toccata à la* Monteverdi as a prelude. Krzysztof Penderecki's *Paradise Lost* (premiered in Chicago in 1978, text by Christopher Fry based on John Milton) is an oratorio-like work that recalls the Renaissance tradition of *rappresentazioni sacre*. The composer, whose early work was in an avant-garde vein and shows his pioneering ventures in new techniques for setting and notation, moved toward more neo-romantic writing, which became one of the mainstreams in contemporary opera composition at the end of the 1970's. Despite the resurgence of romanticism, chromatic, twelve-tone composition also persists, as the successful operas of Aribert Reimann demonstrate. Reimann's *Lear* (premiered in Munich in 1978, libretto by Claus H. Henneberg based on Shakespeare) is one of the

most performed opera works of the last 20 years. Since 1977, the colossal *Licht* (Light) heptalogy (a series of seven works the composer plans to complete by the year 2002) of Karlheinz Stockhausen has evolved out of a trifold row of tones, subdivided into leitmotif-like "formulas." So far, Stockhausen has completed and seen the premieres of five of the operas in the seven-work series he envisions: *Donnerstag aus Licht* (Thursday from Light, Milan 1981), *Samstag aus Licht* (Saturday from Light, Milan, 1984), *Montag aus Licht* (Monday from Light, Milan, 1988), *Dienstag aus Licht* (Tuesday from Light, Leipzig, 1993), and *Freitag aus Licht* (Friday from Light, Leipzig 1996). Stockhausen wrote all the librettos himself. Each new work in the series seems to demand increasing technical complexity from the production and increasing specialization from participants (instrumentalists, dancers, solo voices, choruses), making each new part seem to approach closer and closer to unperformability.

Der junge Lord (The Young Lord), by Hans Werner Henze. Circus scene in the first act of the colorful production by Gustav Rudolf Sellner (Vienna, 1978, staging by Federico Pallavicini). Sellner also directed the premiere. The young lord, supposedly the nephew of the wealthy, newly arrived Sir Edgar, throws teacups around and recites Goethe. The country folk in Hülsdorf-Gotha are enchanted until they discover that the lord is a trained monkey.

The auditorium of the *Semperoper* (*Staatsoper*) in Dresden, opened in 1878, rebuilt in 1985 after it was destroyed during the Second World War. The building preceding it, also designed by Gottfried Semper, was destroyed by fire in 1869.

Almost all theaters erected since the Renaissance have been patterned after the Greek arena: The ground plan is semicircular with ascending rows of seats. In ancient Greece, a small podium (*skene*) closed off the back of the arena (*orchestra*) with a wall (*scenae frons*) designed to look like the front of a house or temple. The *Teatro Olimpico* in Vicenza built at the end of the 16th century was modeled on this style. Its *scenae frons* allowed a view through three doors onto a steep ascending back stage (see p. 12); of course, one could only play on the narrow front of the stage. During the Baroque era, the *scenae frons* disappeared; in its place, scenery was erected, arranged according to the laws of perspective to allow for greater optical depth. The stage itself was also widened: The *Teatro Farnese* in Parma, built in 1618, was 125 feet deep. The spectator area, the auditorium, was often laid out like a horseshoe. The orchestra was placed in the space in front of the stage—the antique "orchestra"—known today as the main floor.

The orchestra pit, which hid the musicians from view, is a relatively recent innovation; it did not appear until the end of the 19th century. The Baroque backdrop stage was followed by the proscenium, or fourth-wall stage, which gives the impression of a closed room, with an invisible "fourth wall" between the action and the audience. The trend in the 20th century has been increasingly away from illusionary stages through efforts to incorporate the audience space into the overall conception of a theater or a specific production. Up until today, opera houses have continued to be built on the model of ascending tiers, which were once arranged in galleries or rows of separate boxes stacked on top of one another. The stage area, which usually exceeds the auditorium in height and volume, can be sealed off from the rest of the theater in a matter of seconds by a so-called iron curtain to conform with fire and safety regulations. The stage opening—that is, the transition between the two parts of the building—is called the portal or proscenium. One of the most important technical advances in theater construction (other than the introduction of electric lighting) has been the revolving stage, which has enabled quick, almost noiseless changes.

Berlin

Since the reunification of Germany in 1990, Berlin has three

Ground plan of the Teatro alla Scala in Milan, opened in 1778. The front rooms house catering and gastronomy; the prince and his family were seated in the center box. Another box at the front, to the left of the stage (number four), was also reserved for the royal family.

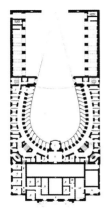

opera houses. The oldest, named after its location "Unter den Linden," was designed by Georg Wenzeslaus von Knobelsdorff. When it opened in 1742, it had room for an audience of about 1000. Rebuilt after World War II, it can now accommodate about 1,400 people. In 1925, Alban Berg's *Wozzeck* was premiered at the Linden Opera.

The *Deutsche Oper Berlin* is a larger building; it seats 1,900. It was erected in 1961 on the site of the former city opera and designed by architect Fritz Bornemann. It has been the home of premieres of Hans Werner Henze's *Der junge Lord* (1966) and Luigi Dallapiccola's *Ulisse* (1968). Besides these two houses, which usually present operas performed in their original language, Berlin is also home to the so-called *Komische Oper*, founded in 1947 with 1,300 seats, traditionally performing works in German.

Dresden

Dresden has one of the world's most famous opera houses and is equally rich in tradition. Since the Baroque era, this city, with its famous, 450-year-old state orchestra has always attracted great composers and conductors, including Richard Wagner and Richard Strauss, whose admiration for this opera house is common knowledge. Correspondingly long, and still growing, is the list of important premieres that have taken place here. Among them are three Wagner operas as well as almost all the operas by Richard Strauss. The original Dresden *Staatsoper* was designed by Gottfried Semper. It was destroyed by bombing during the Second World War but was rebuilt and finally reopened in 1985. The opera house is the home of the annual Dresden Music Festival.

London

London's Royal Opera House Covent Garden was founded in 1732 and, after fires and several restorations and expansions, it can now seat more than 2,000 people. Covent Garden housed the premiere of Weber's *Oberon*, as well as several other world premiers, especially of 20th century works. The second, larger opera house in London is the English National Opera, which performs the international repertoire in English-language versions.

Milan

The *Teatro alla Scala* is the largest (2,000 seats and extra standing room) and most famous opera house in Italy—perhaps in the world. It opened in 1778 and was designed by Giuseppe Piermarini. In the 19th century, it became the international shrine for Italian opera. To singers, singing at the Scala was the pinnacle of their career. A number of prominent conductors, from Franco Faccio to Arturo Toscanini, Tullio Serafin to Carlo Maria Giulini, as well as Claudio Abbado and Riccardo Muti (its current musical director), have contributed to the fine reputation of this house.

New York

The Metropolitan Opera in New York City can look back on a tradition of more than 100 years. Founded in 1883, it moved from its original home on 39th Street to a larger, more splendid theater, complete with murals by Marc Chagall, in Lincoln Center in 1966. The current "Met" has room for about 4,000, with standing room facilities. It has become the stage of superstars, so much so that other opera houses often must adjust their star wages to keep pace with those paid in New York. Among the most important premieres at the Met were Puccini's *Il trittico* and *La fanciulla del West*. New York is also home to the New York City Opera, housed in the smaller New York State Theatre, also in Lincoln Center.

Paris

Since 1989, Parisian opera life has revolved around the giant new *Opéra National de Paris* in the *place de la Bastille*, which has 2,700 seats. Still, the *Grand Opéra*, designed by Charles Garnier and inaugurated in 1875, continues to be *the* Parisian opera house. It seats about 2,200 and is used today primarily by ballet companies. Paris boasts also the *Opéra-Comique* (Salle Favart), which was built in 1898. The *Opéra-Comique* was home to premieres of Claude Debussy's *Pelléas et Mélisande* and Gustave Charpentier's *Louise*.

Salzburg

Opened in 1960, the *Grosses Festspielhaus* in Salzburg, designed by architect Clemens Holzbauer, can hold an audience of about 2,200. More impressive still are the dimensions of the stage, which has a proscenium that can open up to nearly 100

feet and room for an orchestra of 120 musicians. Together with the *Kleines Festspielhaus* and the *Felsenreitschule*, it is home to the venerable Salzburg Festival held every summer. The *Kleines Festspielhaus* was inaugurated in 1927 and has about 1,400 seats, about twice the capacity of the *Salzburger Landestheater*, which has a rich tradition of its own and operates outside the regular Salzburg festival dates.

Vienna

The Vienna *Staatsoper* is in every way the equal of Milan's Scala and New York's Met, with the exception of its ticket prices, which are—believe it or not—even higher than the American theaters. Designed by architects Eduard van der Nüll and Siccard von Siccardsburg, and under construction from 1863 to 1869, the *Staatsoper* was destroyed during World War II and reopened in 1955. Today, it can hold an audience of 2,300, including standing room for 567 people. Regular performances also take place in the Vienna *Volksoper*, built in 1898 (1,300 seats), and in the *Theater an der Wien*, inaugurated in 1801, where Beethoven's *Fidelio* premiered.

Glossary

A cappella: Choral songs without instrumental accompaniment. They were particularly associated with the Sistine Chapel in Rome.

Accompagnato: Recitatives with orchestral accompaniment, as opposed to the *secco* recitatives which were usually accompanied only by the harpsichord.

Alexandrine: Verse of 12 or 13 syllables common to the poetry of areas speaking romance languages.

Alto: Vocal range between tenor and soprano (see *Vocal types*).

Aria: A melody of several parts sung by a single voice with instrumental accompaniment (see also *page 49–50*).

Arioso: A melodious recitative; also a short aria.

Atonality: Conscious avoidance of traditional harmonies (major and minor tonality); impartial use of consonance and dissonance.

Ballad opera: The English precursor of the operetta, often a parody of Italian operas.

Ballet de cour: A court ballet, consisting of numerous *entrées* and a concluding *grand ballet*.

Baritone: The medium range of the male singing voice (see *Vocal types*).

Baritone-Martin: A baritone with the aura of a tenor, reaching high tones with ease and lightness (named after Jean-Blaise Martin, a star of the *opéra comique*).

Bass: The deepest male voice (see *Vocal types*).

Bass-baritone: A bass voice with well-developed higher register.

Basso continuo: Bass part in baroque musical ensembles; see *Thorough bass*.

Belcanto: Ital. "beautiful singing," with especial attention given to purity of tone and precise, artistic vocal technique.

Breeches part: A male role sung by a woman.

Buffo: A male singer specialized in comic roles (bass and tenor buffo); his female counterpart is the *soubrette*.

Canzona: A simple opera aria.

Castrato: A singer whose voice break was negated through an operation of the gonads, so that he retained his youthful alto or soprano.

Cavatina: Usually a two-part aria in which the A section is not repeated as in the Da-capo aria; an arioso at the conclusion of a recitative was called a "cavata" in former times.

Chaconne: An instrumental piece composed on a recurring bass motif.

Chromaticism: Use of non-harmonic half tones that do not belong to the basic musical key.

Cithara: An ancient Greek stringed instrument commonly used to accompany a poet reciting his work.

Glossary

Coloratura: Vocal ornamentation through quick runs, *arpeggios*, trills and interval leaps.

Comédie-ballet: French mixed genre, consisting of a play and a ballet.

Commedia dell'arte: Classic Italian improvised comedy with typical roles.

Couleur-locale: Music and scenery imbued with local coloring.

Counterpoint: Polyphonic style of composition in which the different voices are melodically independent and often progress in opposite directions.

Countertenor: A male voice in alto range, a part of English musical tradition.

Couplet: Vocal piece from French operettas consisting of numerous stanzas.

Da-capo aria: Aria repeating the opening section with ornamentation.

Deus ex machina: Sudden intervention of a divine being in the action of the play, often very effectively staged through the use of elaborate theater techniques.

Diatonic: Progression of tones according to the seven tone intervals of the major and minor scales (as opposed to the chromatic scale).

Divertissement: Song and dance interludes in French plays and operas.

Dodecaphonism: Composition based upon the twelve half tones of the chromatic scale (see *Twelve-tone technique*).

Dramma giocoso: Italian comic opera.

Dramma per musica: Serious Italian operas of the 18th century.

Duet: Vocal piece for two solo voices.

Ensemble: A group of musicians or a scene with several singers.

Epilogue: A concluding section to a play.

Falsetto: High male vocal range; with careful training of the falsetto (head voice), men can sing alto and even soprano parts.

Favola in musica: A name for early Italian operas.

Figurine: Costume design or model drawing of a particular role.

Finale: Final scene of an opera or an act.

Fugue: Artful polyphonic composition, developed from a single theme recurring successively in each of the parts or voices.

Full score: Clearly laid out notation and directions for all voices and instruments taking part in a composition.

Gesamtkunstwerk: Theater works that aim at more than a mere connection between music and drama, striving to embody a complete unity of the arts.

Grand opéra: An elaborately staged serious French opera of the 19th century.

Instrumental theater: To play or make music as a theatrical act; all the elements involved in the scene become a part of the composition.

Intermedio: Scenic-musical interlude

between the acts of a play.

Intermezzo: A comic short opera in two or three scenes, placed into an opera seria as an interlude.

Leitmotif: Series of tones or chords that characterize a person or situation, functioning as a recurrent musical symbol.

Libretto: The text of an opera.

Lieto fine: The "happy end" of a baroque opera.

Madrigal: Unaccompanied choral song on a secular text.

Magic opera: An opera in which supernatural characters and magical stage props play an important role (for example, in *Armide*).

Melisma: Several melody tones sung on one text syllable, in contrast to one tone per syllable (as is the case, for example, in a recitative).

Melodrama: Recitation or pantomime with instrumental interpolations or with instrumental accompaniment; a melodram for

one or two characters is referred to as a "monodram" or "duodram" respectively.

Messa di voce: The swelling and diminishing of the voice as a means of expression essential to the bel canto.

Mezzavoce: Sung with half a voice.

Mezzo soprano: Female vocal range between alto and soprano (see *Vocal types*).

Monody: A solo song accompanied by thorough bass.

Moresca: Grotesque, pantomimed dance (Moor dance), also sword dances that portrayed the conflict between the Christians and the Moors (*moriscos*).

Motet: Choral piece, mainly a cappella, mostly on a Latin, religious text.

Musical theater: General term for modern operas and similar scenic-musical productions.

Musica nova: The musical avant-garde of all times,

in particular since 1945.

Musikdrama: The "Gesamtkunstwerk" opera; when narrowly defined: Richard Wagner's completely through-composed operas.

Numbers opera: An opera structured on arias, choruses, and ballets, in which each piece forms in itself a complete and independent musical work; the opposite of the through-composed opera.

Opera buffa: A comic Italian opera of the 18th and early 19th century containing recitatives.

Opéra comique: A French opera with spoken dialogues.

Opera semiseria: An opera genre between the comic and serious.

Opera seria: The main genre of Italian baroque operas, usually on a historical or mythological subject.

Operetta: Musical comedy with spoken dialogues; grew out of

Glossary

vaudeville and opéra comique.

Oratorio: Works for solo voices, chorus and orchestra, originally on religious subjects, later also on secular topics.

Overture: Orchestral piece at the beginning of an opera, also as an introductory movement at the beginning of an instrumental work of several parts.

Parlando: Smoothly flowing declamation, close to the rhythm of ordinary spoken language but akin to song.

Passacaglia: Variations on a continuously repeated (bass) motif.

Pasticcio: A musical composition put together from various pieces of different origins.

Pastorale: Composition or poetry idealizing the shepherd's life and rural ways.

People's opera: Popular opera with elements of folk music, folk costumes etc.; also a term for opera houses which attract a wide audience, in contrast to the court operas with their limited public.

Pléiade: Circle of French poets of the 16th century, named after the illustrious group of seven tragic poets of ancient Alexandria (3rd century BC).

Polyphony: Two or more equal and independent voice parts sounding against each other, in contrast to homophony which consists of a single melody line with subordinate, accompanying voices.

Polytonality: Simultaneous use of different musical keys.

Prima ballerina: First solo dancer in a ballet company.

Prima donna: Female opera star, singer of the main roles of (Italian) operas; her male counterpart is the *primo uomo*; *prima donna assoluta* is a female singer who has mastered the coloratura, both the lyrical and the dramatic; the singer of the second main role is referred to as *seconda donna*,

or *second'uomo* respectively.

Program music: Music that seeks to portray incidents outside of the realm of music, for example, through the imitation of natural occurrences.

Prologue: Scenic preface.

Prosody: The study of accents or metrical structures in verse.

Rappresentazione sacra: Religious play with music.

Recitative: Syllabic song in operas which grew out of the *stile recitativo* of monody; *recitativo accompagnato* with numerous orchestral instruments; *recitativo secco* with only thorough bass instruments and/ or harpsichord accompaniment.

Rescue opera: Operas depicting the rescue of the main personage(s) from a hopeless situation.

Ritornello: Instrumental interlude or a short recurrent musical passage (for example, in an aria).

Glossary

Romance: A simple often sentimental strophic song in the French tradition.

Rondo: A composition consisting of a recurring theme and different interludes (basic structure: a-b-a-c-a-d-a etc.).

Scrittura: Opera commission (Italian).

Semi opera: Opera with spoken dialogues (English).

Serial music: Music based on the twelve-tone technique, defining in addition parameters such as tone length, tone coloring, dynamics etc. to construct musical sequences.

Singspiel: German term for a primarily comic play with music, close to such folk comedies as a "Schwank" or "Posse;" in contrast to the *opera buffa*, the *singspiel* characteristically has spoken dialogues.

Song: English term for song, ballad, or poem, used also in German speaking areas since Brecht/Weill.

Soprano: Highest female voice range (see also *Vocal types*).

Sprechgesang: Speechsong, speaking according to an (approximately) prescribed melody.

Tenor: High male vocal range (see *Vocal types*).

Tessitura: The tonal range of a vocal piece and the demands implied thereby.

Thorough bass: A technique of composition common to the baroque. Only the melody line and the bass notes were written down; the middle voices were improvised. A system of numbers delineated the harmonic progressions.

Timbre: Characteristic tonal color or quality of a (singing) voice.

Toccata: A musical composition, not structurally defined, close to a fantasia, often alternating chords with very fast passages.

Tragédie lyrique: A serious French opera of the 17th and 18th centuries.

Trio: Vocal piece for three solo voices or a three member (vocal) ensemble, further quartet, quintet, sextet etc.

Trionfo: An elaborate, celebratory procession in the Italian Renaissance.

Twelve-tone technique (Twelve-tone music): Compositions based on the twelve half tones of the chromatic scale, whereby all intervals are equally relevant; this technique is based on Arnold Schönberg's theory of twelve tones which are related only to each other.

Vaudeville: French popular melody, also a term for musical comedies; in the so-called vaudeville finale, the ensemble members stand in a row facing the audience and proclaim the moral of the story (for example, *The Abduction from the Seraglio*).

Verismo: A particular version of naturalism in Italian operas.

Zarzuela: Comic Spanish opera, Spanish *singspiel*.

Zeitoper, "topical opera": Operas which concern themselves with contemporaneous events, as opposed to historical and mythological subjects.

Picture credits

Vocal Types

Vocal types

Well-trained voices have a range of about two octaves, so that each range somewhat overlaps with the adjacent ones. Six basic distinctions are made (the approximate tonal expanse is noted in parentheses).

Soprano (h–h'', high sopranos reach such peak tones as f''')
Mezzo soprano (a–a'')
Alto (f–f'')
Tenor (H–h', by far not all tenors can reach a c'', the so-called high C)
Baritone (G–g')
Bass (E–e', few basses reach the deep C).

In the opera profession, it is common to categorize voices into vocal groups or types, but not only the range but also the timbre of the voice determine its suitability for certain roles (in parentheses, a typical role for each type and range of voice is noted).

Coloratura soprano (Susanna, *Marriage of Figaro*)
Dramatic coloratura soprano (Queen of the Night, *Magic Flute*)
Lyrical soprano (Pamina, *Magic Flute*)
Youthful, dramatic soprano (Desdemona, *Otello*)
Dramatic soprano (Santuzza, *Cavalleria rusticana*)
Highly dramatic soprano (Isolde, *Tristan und Isolde*)
Coloratura mezzo soprano (Rosina, *Il Barbiere di Siviglia*)
Dramatic mezzo soprano (Amneris, *Aida*)
Lyrical mezzo soprano (Maddalena, *Rigoletto*)

Lyrical tenor (Don Ottavio, *Don Giovanni*)
Youthful heroic tenor (Florestan, *Fidelio*)
Heroic tenor (Siegfried, *Ring of the Nibelung*)
Tenor buffo (David, *Meistersinger*)
Heroic baritone (Wotan, *Ring of the Nibelung*)
Cavalier baritone (Don Giovanni, *Don Giovanni*)
Serious bass (Sarastro, *Magic Flute*)
Playful bass (Leporello, *Don Giovanni*)
Bass buffo (Ochs, *Rosenkavalier*)

Usually singers go through different vocal types during their career, and it is equally common to change from one vocal range into a neighboring one (for example, from alto to mezzo or from bass to baritone).

Survey of Important Dates in Opera History

Survey of important dates in opera history

(P = premiere)

1480 The drama *Fabula d'Orfeo* by Angelo Poliziano premiered in Mantua.

1598 Jacopo Peri's *Dafne* premiered in Florence (music has been lost).

1600 P of *Euridice* by Peri in Florence.

1602 P of *Euridice* by Giulio Caccini in Florence (Palazzo Pitti).

1607 P of *L'Orfeo* by Claudio Monteverdi in Mantua.

1619 P of *La morte d'Orfeo* by Stefano Landi in Rome.

1627 Heinrich Schütz' *Daphne*, the first German oper (now lost) had its premiere in Torgau.

1637 The first public opera house, the Teatro San Cassiano, opened in Venice.

1643 P of *L'incoronazione di Poppea* by Monteverdi at the Teatro Santi Giovanni e Paolo in Venice.

1643 Death of Monteverdi in Venice (November 29).

1662 *L'ercole amante* by Francesco Cavalli with choruses and ballets by Jean-Baptiste Lully had its premiere in the Salle des Machines of the Tuileries in Paris

1668 Opening of the opera house on the Cortina in Vienna with a production of *Il pomo d'oro* by Antonio Cesti.

1678 Opening of the *Oper am Gänsemarkt* in Hamburg.

1685 Georg Friedrich Handel born in Halle/Saale on February 23.

1687 Jean-Baptiste Lully dies in Paris (March 22).

1689 P of *Dido and Aeneas* by Henry Purcell in the boarding school for girls in Chelsea run by the dancing master Josias Priest.

1698 Birth of Pietro Metastasio in Rome on January 3.

1711 Handel's *Rinaldo* premieres at the London Haymarket (Queen's Theater).

1724 The castrato Farinelli (Carlo Broschi) gives his debut in Vienna.

1733 P of *La serva padrona* by Giovanni Battista Pergolesi in Naples.

1735 P of *Les indes galantes*, ballet opera by Jean-Philippe Rameau.

1746 First Paris performance of *La serva padrona*.

1752 Jean-Jacques Rousseau composes *Le devin du village*.

1756 Birth of Wolfgang Amadeus Mozart in Salzburg on January 27.

1778 The *Teatro alla Scala* opens in Milan.

1786 P of *Doktor und Apotheker* by Karl Ditters von Dittersdorf in Vienna.

1787 P of *Don Giovanni* by Mozart at the *Gräflich Nostitzsches Nationaltheater* in Prague.

1797 P of *Médée* by Luigi Cherubini at the *Théâtre Feydeau* in Paris.

1805 P of *Fidelio* by Ludwig van Beethoven.

1813 Birth of Richard Wagner (May 22) and Giuseppe Verdi (October 10).

Survey of Important Dates in Opera History

1826 P of Carl Maria von Weber's *Oberon* in London (Covent Garden).

1829 P of *Guillaume Tell* by Gioacchino Rossini in Paris.

1836 P of *A Life for the Tsar* by Mikhail Glinka at the Imperial Theater in St. Petersburg.

1842 P of *Nabucco* by Verdi at the Scala in Milan.

1850 P of *Lohengrin* by Wagner at the Weimar court theater.

1864 Ludwig II of Bavaria assures Wagner of his generous support.

1876 Wagner's *Ring of the Nibelung* premieres in the newly erected *Festspielhaus* in Bayreuth.

1881 Opening of the National Theater in Prague with Bedřich Smetana's *Libussa*.

1893 P of *Falstaff* by Verdi at the Scala in Milan.

1900 P of *Tosca* by Giacomo Puccini in Rome (Teatro Costanzi).

1902 P of *Pelléas et Mélisande* by Claude Debussy in Paris (Salle Favart).

1905 P of *Salome* by Richard Strauss in Dresden (Semper-Oper).

1913 *The Rite of Spring* (scenes from heathen Russia), a ballet by Igor Stravinsky.

1920 First Salzburg Festival takes place.

1925 P of *Wozzeck* by Alban Berg in Berlin (Staats-oper).

1934 Founding of the summer opera festival in Glyndebourne.

1935 P of *Porgy and Bess* by George Gershwin in New York (Alvin Theater).

1945 P of *Peter Grimes* by Benjamin Britten in London (Sadler's Wells Theater).

1947 Founding of the Comic Opera in Berlin.

1949 Death of Richard Strauss in Garmisch (September 8).

1951 P of *The Rake's Progress* by Igor Stravinsky in Venice (La Fenice).

1959 P of *Aniara* by Karl-Birger Blomdahl in Stockholm, the portrayal of men fleeing in a spaceship from the earth after its contamination through radio-activity.

1965 P of *Die Soldaten* by Bernd Alois Zimmermann in Cologne.

1966 Inauguration of the Metropolitan Opera House in New York (Lincoln Center) with a production of *Anthony and Cleopatra* by Samuel Barber.

1971 P of *Staats-theater* by Mauricio Kagel in Hamburg.

1977 Death of Maria Callas in Paris (September 16).

1985 Re-opening of the Semper-Oper in Dresden.

1992 P of *Die Eroberung von Mexiko* by Wolfgang Rihm in Hamburg.

Bibliography

Barzun, Jacques.
Berlioz and the Romantic Century. 2 vols. Boston: Little, Brown, 1950.

Beauvert, Thierry.
Opera Houses of the World. London: Thames and Hudson, 1996.

Blyth, Alan. *Opera on Video.* London: Kyle Cathie, 1995.

Boyden, Matthew.
Opera: The Rough Guide. London: The Rough Guides, 1997.

Brook, Stephen. *Opera: A Penguin Anthology.* New York: Viking, 1995.

Brower, Harriette, and **James Francis Cooke.** *Great Singers on the Art of Singing.* Mineola, NY: Dover, 1996.

Caruso, Dorothy, and **Torrance Goddard.** *Wings of Song: The Story of Caruso.* New York: Minton, Balch, and Co., 1928.

Caruso, Enrico, Jr., and **Andrew Farkas.** *My Father and My Family.* Portland, OR: Amadeus Press, 1997.

Csampai, Attila, ed. *Callas: Images of a Legend.* London: Stewart Tabori and Chang, 1996.

Conrad, Peter. *A Song of Love and Death: The Meaning of Opera.* St. Paul, MN: Graywolf, 1996.

Cord, William O. *An Introduction to Richard Wagner's Der Ring des Nibelungen.* Columbus: Ohio University Press, 1995.

Dean, Winton. *Essays on Opera.* New York: Oxford University Press, 1990.

Dent, Edward Joseph. *The Rise of Romantic Opera.* New York: Cambridge University Press, 1976.

Dizikes, John. *Opera in America: A Cultural History.* New Haven, CT: Yale University Press, 1993.

Gishford, Anthony, ed. "Introduction" by Benjamin Britten. *Grand Opera: The Story of the World's Leading Opera Houses and Personalities.* New York: Viking, 1972.

Goldovsky, Boris. *Bringing Opera to Life.* New York: Appleton-Century-Crofts, 1968.

Graf, Herbert. *The Opera and Its Future in America.* New York: W.W. Norton, 1941.

Heartz, Daniel, ed. *Mozart's Operas.* Berkeley: University of California Press, 1990.

Heriot, Angus. *The Castrati in Opera.* London: Da Capo, 1975.

Hunter, Mary Kathleen. *The Culture of Opera Buffa in Mozart's Vienna: A Poetics of Entertainment.* Princeton, NJ: Princeton University Press, 1998.

Jarman, Douglas. *The Music of Alban Berg.* Berkeley: University of California, 1979.

Lindenberger, Herbert. *Opera in History: From Monteverdi to Cage.* Stanford, CA: Stanford University Press, 1998.

Morden, Ethan. *Opera Anecdotes.* Oxford: Oxford University Press, 1985.

Bibliography

The New Grove. Volumes include (among others): Twentieth Century American Masters; Modern Masters; Russian Masters 1; Second Viennese School; Masters of Italian Opera. New York: W.W. Norton, various years.

Newman, Ernest. T*he Life of Richard Wagner.* 3 vols. New York: Knopf, 1933.

Osborne, Charles. *The Complete Operas of Mozart: A Critical Guide.* New York: Da Capo, 1988. Other composers in this series include: Puccini (1983), Richard Strauss (1991), Richard Wagner (1993), and Verdi (1988).

Plaut, Eric A. *Grand Opera: Mirror of the Western Mind.* Chicago: Ivan R. Dee, 1993.

Rademacher, Johannes. *Music: An Illustrated Historical Overview.* Hauppauge, NY: Barron's Educational Series, 1996.

Radice, Mark, ed. *Opera in Context: Essays on Historical Staging from the late Renaissance to the Time of Puccini.* Portland, OR: Amadeus Press, 1998.

Robinson, Michael F. *Opera Before Mozart.* New York: William Morrow, 1966.

Robinson, Paul. *Opera and Ideas: From Mozart to Strauss.* New York: Harper and Row, 1985.

Sabor, Rudolph. *Der Ring des Nibelungen: A Companion.* San Francisco: Phaidon/Chronicle, 1997.

Sadie, Stanley, ed. *The New Grove Book of Operas.* New York: St. Martin's Press, 1997.

Schmidgall, Gary. *Literature as Opera.* New York: Oxford University Press, 1977.

Schmidgall, Gary. *Shakespeare and Opera.* New York: Oxford University Press, 1990.

Spotts, Frederic. *Bayreuth: A History of the Wagner Festival.* New Haven, CT: Yale University Press, 1994.

Stendhal. *Life of Rossini.* New York: Orion, 1970.

Strohm, Richard. *Dramma Per Musica: Italian Opera Seria of the Eighteenth Century.* New Haven, CT: Yale University Press, 1997.

Stuckenschmidt, H. H. *Schoenberg: His Life, World, and Work,* trans. by Humphrey Searle. New York: Schirmer, 1977.

Sutcliffe, Tom. *Believing in Opera.* Princeton, NJ: Princeton University Press, 1997.

Van Gilles, De. *Verdi's Theater: Creating Drama through Music,* trans. by Gilda Roberts. Chicago: University of Chicago Press, 1998.

Wagner, Richard. *Opera and Drama,* trans. by W. Ashton Ellis. Lincoln: University of Nebraska Press, 1995.

Waugh, Alexander. *Opera: A New Way of Listening.* London: De Agostini, 1996.

Weaver, William. *The Golden Century of Italian Opera: From Rossini to Puccini.* London: Thames and Hudson, 1980.

Index of Names

Index of Names

Index of Names

Index of Names

Index of Names

Index of Names

Index of Composers and Their Works

Index of Composers and Their Works

Index of Composers and Their Works

Index of Composers and Their Works

Index of Composers and Their Works

Index of Composers and Their Works

Index of Composers and Their Works

Index of Composers and Their Works